# THE
# TEMPLE

## The Place of God

by
John Chitham

ISBN No: 978-1-907636-31-8

Published by Verité CM Ltd

Cover design, typesetting and production management by
Verité CM Ltd, Worthing, West Sussex UK
+44 (0) 1903 241975

Printed in England

Dedication

I dedicate this book to my wife Basma.
Through her I have had a unique experience of Middle Eastern
culture which has informed much of what is written.
But far beyond that without her love, support and
encouragement much more than just this book
would be missing from my life

# Contents

# Introduction and Acknowledgements

Writing a book about the temple in the Bible has been a joy. It has taken me to unexpected places and revealed new aspects of God's word. It has helped me understand more of what the Holy Spirit is telling us in the scriptures and also directed my ongoing discipleship.

The spur to consider the continuing importance of the temple came from G. K. Beale's book, "The Temple and the Church's Mission"[1] which is the basis for the underlying theology in many of the chapters. I recommend it wholeheartedly for anyone who wishes to go deeper into the issue of the tabernacle/temple. There are a number of other theological influences that may be apparent for many readers. Chief among these is the work of Tom Wright although there are many others, conscious and unconscious. A different kind of inspiration has come from books by authors that quote parts of scripture and then have an applied commentary on them. These include William Temple (on John's Gospel), William Barclay and Tom Wright. But this is to mention the greats; the only comparison I make is to do with concept, not quality.

There is an important difference from those commentaries. This book follows a theme rather than one biblical book. This lays me open to a criticism of selection and omission. However the further I have gone into the subject the more I have realised it is impossible to be complete. My criterion for selection is primarily theological, that the temple is defined as the place of God. It has also been to do with personal interest and inspiration. Others may be inspired by God through the Holy Spirit by other texts: to him be the glory!

My thanks need to go to many people for this even seeing the light of day. Some chapters originated in sermons given to congregations in Worthing: I am very grateful to the people of Holy Trinity, Christ Church and especially St. Matthew's for their comments and encouragements over the years. Thanks also need to be given in particular to Laya Burgan (like the line of David, she

---

[1] G. K. Beale, *The Temple and the Church's Mission*, New Studies in Biblical Theology 17, IVP 2004

too is part Moabite and part Bethlehemite!) for the line drawings produced for each chapter. Chris Powell has been generous in his support for publication.

# Schematic map of the Tabernacle

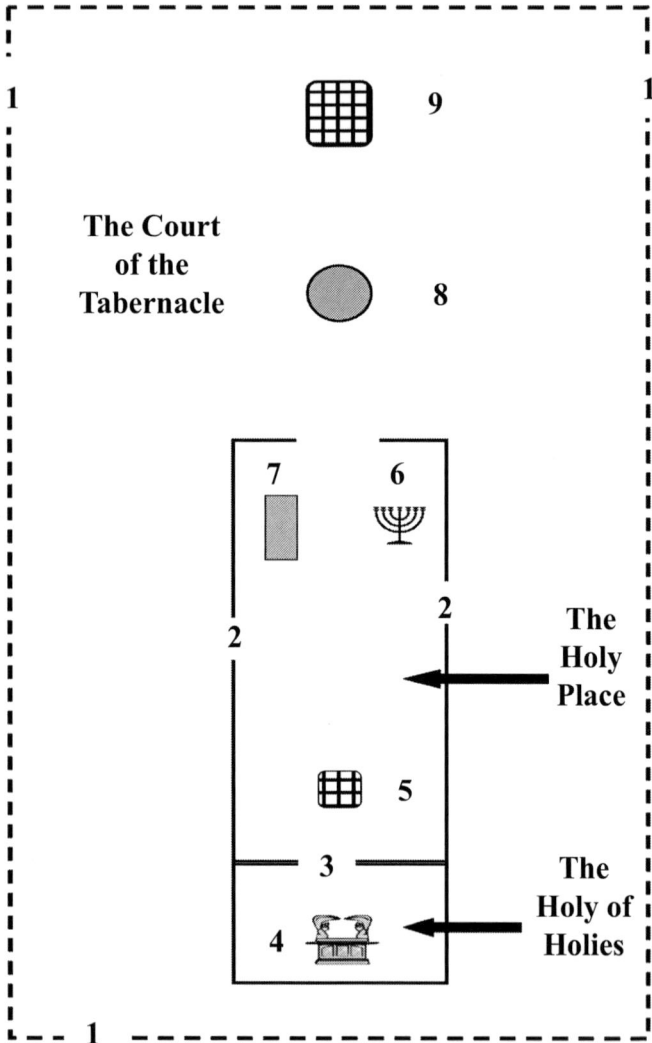

**1**            **9**           **1**

**The Court
of the
Tabernacle**      **8**

**7**     **6**

**2**       **2**

**The
Holy
Place**

**5**

**3**

**The
Holy of
Holies**

**4**

**1**                **1**

1 The Fence around the Tabernacle      5 The Altar of Incense
2 The Edge of the Tent      6 The Menorah
3 The Curtain      7 The Table of Shewbread
4 The Ark of the Covenant in the Holy of Holies      8 The Laver
     9 The Altar

# Schematic map of the Herodian Temple

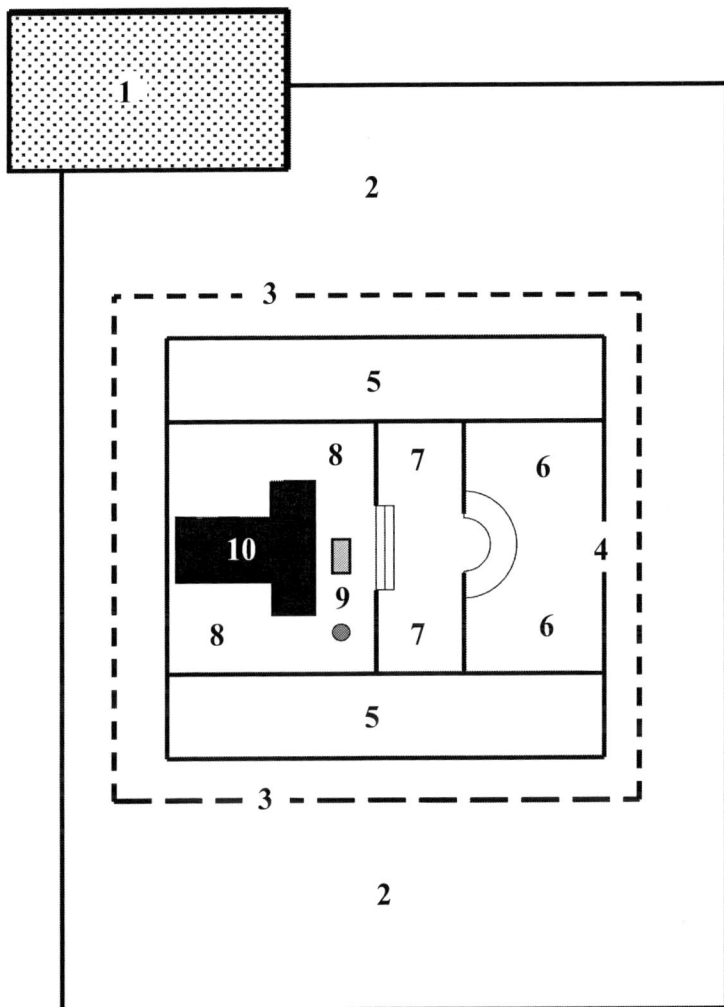

1 The Antonia Fortress (Roman)
2 The Court of the Gentiles
3 The Balustrade
4 Main Entrance
5 Various Rooms, Storage
6 The Court of Women

7 The Court of Israel (for Jewish men)
8 The Court of the Priests
9 The Altar and Laver
10 The Sanctuary (the sanctuary was very impressive but the floor plan was similar to the Tabernacle, except that there was a second curtain at the entrance)

# 1. The Place of God

*Isaiah 66:1-2*

*¹This is what the LORD says: "Heaven is my throne, and the earth is my footstool. Where is the house you will build for me? Where will my resting place be? ²Has not my hand made all these things, and so they came into being?" declares the LORD. "This is the one I esteem: he who is humble and contrite in spirit, and trembles at my word..."*

*1 Corinthians 3:9-*

*⁹For we are God's fellow-workers; you are God's field, God's building. ¹⁰By the grace God has given me, I laid a foundation as an expert builder, and someone else is building on it. But each one should be careful how he builds. ¹¹For no-one can lay any foundation other than the one already laid, which is Jesus Christ. ¹²If any man builds on this foundation using gold, silver, costly stones, wood, hay or straw, ¹³his work will be shown for what it is, because the Day will bring it to light. It will be revealed with fire, and the fire will test the quality of each man's work. ¹⁴If what he has built survives, he will receive his reward. ¹⁵If it is burned up, he will suffer loss; he himself will be saved, but only as one escaping through the flames. ¹⁶Don't you know that you yourselves are God's temple and that God's Spirit lives in you? ¹⁷If anyone destroys God's temple, God will destroy him; for God's temple is sacred, and you are that temple.*

If you wanted to study a topic in the scriptures that focussed, in some way, the whole message of God to humanity, what would it be? Certainly all references to the Messiah, the Christ, would do it; perhaps also a close study of the events that began on Palm Sunday and finished at Pentecost. Probably one could

study certain words, such as salvation, as long as one looked at the background enough. God's revelation of himself in the scriptures is a little like a room with many windows; choose the right window, and one gets a complete view. However one window that few would think to choose is that of the temple. In the analogy it is a little like a rather cob-webbed window obscured through lack of use. Yet I am convinced that a thorough study of the temple in the scriptures is as good a way as any of coming to grips with all the major themes of the Bible. A study of the temple will give a unique viewpoint on what God has shown us.

Why is the temple such an unpopular and unlikely theme today? In the past, it was indeed one of the major topics for preachers. This is reinforced by fact that many Protestant churches in Victorian times were called "tabernacle", and that popular drawings and models were of the furnishings and layout of both the tabernacle and the first century temple.

Therein lies part of the problem. The image of the study of the temple is reduced to maps and furnishings which seem to have obscure and not very appealing symbolism. Added to this is a trawl through some of the most uninviting parts of the Pentateuch. Modern western people are much more interested in stories and ethics than in architecture wrapped up in difficult writing.

This book will, of necessity, look at some of that. However it is not the only, nor indeed the prominent, strand to the study of the temple. The temple is as much New Testament as Old, as much Revelation as Moses, and more Jesus and the Church than any of them. The reason I can say this is the working definition for the temple: the temple is **the place of God**.

The temple is where God resides. The temple in the scriptures is a progressive revelation of God and his dealing with humanity. Studying the temple is not just about the physical structures. Of these physical structures there was the temple built by Solomon, the temple built when the Israelites returned from exile in Babylon, and the temple built by King Herod in Jesus' time. One can also add to that the tent (the tabernacle) which the Israelites faithfully carried through the desert after they left Egypt. These are the four temples built by human hands and which, one by one, were destroyed in various ways.

Yet these are by no means all the temples mentioned in Bible. A glance through a concordance will give you others. In Acts 7 Stephen quotes Isaiah 66:1,2: "What kind of house will you build for me?...Has not my hand made these things?" As we shall see later in this book, the point is that a temple made by hand is, in the last analysis, inadequate for God, however closely his instructions are followed. It can lead to idolatry and this was one of the main reasons Stephen was stoned to death.

The temple was also one of the main reasons why Jesus was crucified. "Destroy this temple and I will raise it again in three days", he said, on the Temple Mount. This statement was twisted and used against him at his trial. Nevertheless the disciples recognised that he was speaking about himself (John 2:19-23). Jesus identified himself with the temple.

In 1 Corinthians 6:19 Paul says: "Do you not know that your body is a temple of the Holy Spirit, who is in you?" Paul does say "*a* temple" rather than "*the* temple"; nevertheless he is directly associating the temple of God with an individual believer.

Earlier in the letter he speaks of the Corinthian church as a whole as God's temple. "Don't you know that you are God's temple and that God's Spirit lives within you?" (1 Corinthians 3:16). There is no lack of clarity here. Paul is speaking of the very temple of his God, before the one in Jerusalem had been destroyed.

The New Testament, even in this brief survey, speaks of the temple being impossible to be made by hands, as being Jesus the Christ, *and* the individual believer *and* a local body of believers. It is tempting to assume that these are metaphors, that the real temple was the building in Jerusalem and that these were comparisons drawing on the temple for their meaning. But why should this be so? The combination of identities above is striking and convincing. The true temple is where God resides, not where there is a building. A building as such could never be that, unless God were there. The basis of the temple is God, not a building. Jesus, and Stephen his follower, were killed for saying or implying that God was not dwelling in the Jerusalem temple.

These three examples of the temple (the believer, the church and Jesus himself) are foundational. Let me give two examples of my own. In my travels in the Middle East I have seen striking examples of each. Once I visited a man in the poorer area of Damascus, with a local pastor and a famous British preacher. It seemed a bit of an imposition at the time, but as often happens; God turned our inconvenience into wonder. The man was a convert from Islam and was crippled. The house had two small rooms and his "bedroom" was an alcove. He could hardly leave his mattress for long. His mother looked after him. In summer the house would have been an oven, with the outside temperature over 40° C. Yet he had a ministry in writing. He developed his network in various ways and wrote, testifying to the joy of Jesus. This ministry was bearing fruit, but that was not the most striking thing. It was the man himself. In translated Arabic and broken English, we heard the voice of one indwelled by the Holy Spirit. Here was one who glowed with God, despite his poverty and affliction.

In my house I have a quiet room, where I go to pray. One of my aids to prayer is an icon, known as the *pantocrator*. It is an image of Christ as the ruler of the universe, his hand raised in blessing, and the other hand holding the gospel. As it happens, this too is from Damascus. I find it useful as a way of coming to Christ and worshipping him (not, of course, the icon itself). The point is that the icon leads me towards the glory of Christ, who is the fullness of God. It leads me to the one who sits on the throne in the heavenly Jerusalem, where there is no need for a temple.

It is often objected at this point that God is Spirit and omnipresent. The reason why the temple is no longer relevant is that God has deliberately moved from having one special place and one special, tribal people to be open to everyone, everywhere. There is truth in that. God is omnipresent, and his salvation is open to Gentiles as well as Jews. The Holy Spirit came down at Pentecost and now works his will in his world. Nevertheless, God does still promise himself in certain situations: as we cach, as individuals, are born again; in the fellowship of others; supremely, as we meet Jesus. In those senses, the temple remains today. It is a continuation and development of the temples of the Old Testament.

Suddenly the study of the temple becomes much wider in our understanding: it is the place of the presence of God, where he dwells in his majesty. A study on where God is must be of the utmost importance to all Christians. We want to be with him and worship him. How can we do that unless we know his presence?

The Old Testament temples remain the pattern, the template for the post-Jesus temple. A study of those temples will make us aware of the temple today, and in the future. For there is another temple in the New Testament, that of Revelation 21:22, "I did not see a temple in the city, because the Lord God almighty and the Lamb are its temple." Supremely, here, we see the definition of the temple to come, and as it always has been: the presence of God.

This is the reason why the temple is a place of worship. It is the reason why we worship Jesus: he is God. It is the reason why we respect ("worship") our bodies: God's Holy Spirit is there. It is why we worship in the company of other believers (and not necessarily in a building): God is present.

Where God is, certain things are bound to follow: a sense of penitence, because we are unworthy; a sense of sacrifice, because he demands it; a sense of liberation, because he frees; a sense of joy; because he saves; a sense of wonder, because he is wonderful; a sense of glory, because he is glorious. In our studies on the temple, the full revelation of God in the scriptures will come into view. It is an exciting ride.

## Questions to consider

What difference does it make that you are a temple of the Holy Spirit?

Where do you go to find God?

How does God come to you?

# 2. The First Temple

*Genesis 2:8-12, 15-16; 3:24*

   [8]*Now the LORD God had planted a garden in the east, in Eden; and there he put the man he had formed. [9]And the LORD God made all kinds of trees grow out of the ground—trees that were pleasing to the eye and good for food. In the middle of the garden were the tree of life and the tree of the knowledge of good and evil. [10]A river watering the garden flowed from Eden; from there it was separated into four headwaters. [11]The name of the first is the Pishon; it winds through the entire land of Havilah, where there is gold. [12](The gold of that land is good; aromatic resin and onyx are also there.)... [15]The LORD God took the man and put him in the Garden of Eden to work it and take care of it. [16]And the LORD God commanded the man... [24]After he drove the man out, he placed on the east side of the Garden of Eden cherubim and a flaming sword flashing back and forth to guard the way to the tree of life.*

*Exodus 25:7, 18, 31*

   [7]*Onyx stones and other gems (are) to be mounted on the ephod and breastpiece... [18]And make two cherubim out of hammered gold...[31]make a lampstand of pure gold and hammer it out, base and shaft; its flowerlike cups, buds and blossoms shall be of one piece with it.*

*Revelation 22:1-3*

   [1]*Then the angel showed me the river of the water of life, as clear as crystal, flowing from the throne of God and of the Lamb [2]down the middle of the great street of the city. On each side of the river stood the tree of life...and the leaves of the tree are for the healing of the nations. [3]No longer will there be any curse.*

The Omayyad Mosque in Damascus, built in the early eighth century, has some of the most extraordinary mosaics in the world. They stretch all around the walls of the interior of the huge courtyard using only green and gold. They show groves, orchards, fields, rivers, pavilions and palaces. There is not a human being or animal to be seen, following the Islamic ruling not to show living beings. However the workmanship was entrusted largely to the local Christians who were experts in mosaics. The vision presented is not merely Islamic, but Christian also. As people come to worship God it shows that paradise like the Garden of Eden.

The first temple was the Garden of Eden. If the temple is the place where God dwells, then above all other places the Garden is a temple. If we look at the Old Testament temples we can see that they deliberately copied the Garden of Eden.

We can see it first of all in some of the detail of the temple. The lampstand of the temple was made to look like a flowering tree, probably representing the tree of life. Elsewhere in the temple there was furniture carved with "gourds and open flowers" (1 Kings 6:18), "palm trees and open flowers" (1 Kings 6:29) and pomegranates (1 Kings 7:20), among other examples. This most likely represents the foliage of the Garden. By the Ark of the Covenant there were two cherubim, similar to the cherubim guarding the entrance to the Garden. The ephod of the priest had onyx and other gems, as did the land of Havilah, which was part of or next to the Garden. This land also had good gold, and the lampstand, cherubim, and other artefacts, were made of gold.

Second, the entrance to the temple is always on the east, just as the cherubim guarded the east side of Eden. Ezekiel describes the final temple as also having an eastern entrance (Ezekiel 40:6).

Third, Adam worshipped in the Garden. This does not appear at first sight in the English translations of the Bible, but it does in Hebrew. Adam was commanded to "cultivate and keep" the Garden. Elsewhere these same words are translated "serve and guard", in the context of the Israelites serving God and guarding (keeping)

God's word, or the priests "keeping" the service. No doubt there was real gardening that Adam did, but this manual labour should be seen as maintaining the order of the sanctuary. This view is the one taken by many Jewish commentators between the Testaments. This worship is immediately followed by a command, to eat of any tree, but not the tree of the knowledge of good and evil. The later temples are the place where the commands of God are kept, or else there will be grave consequences (e.g. 1 Kings 9:6-7). However it is in the Garden where the first command was issued.

Fourth, the temple is the source of water. Whilst there were not streams flowing from the temples and tabernacle, all of the descriptions of the temple to come have water flowing from them, the river of life in Ezekiel 47, Zechariah 14 and Revelation 21.

Finally, and perhaps above all, both the Garden and the temple are the place of God's rest. God rested after the six days of creation (Genesis 2:1); the temple is God's resting place forever, "This is my resting place forever; here I dwell, for I have desired it" (Psalm 132:14-15).

There are other possible similarities that could be mentioned but perhaps this is enough for now. The temple is planned along the lines of the Garden; the Garden is the first temple, the pattern from which the others are simply copies.

Where does this leave us today? So what if the first temple is the Garden of Eden? It is a while ago now, but in the late sixties and early seventies Joni Mitchell had two songs out, called "Big Yellow taxi" and "Woodstock"[1]. These are some of the lyrics:

*"Big Yellow Taxi"*
    They took all the trees
    And put them in a tree museum
    And they charged all the people
    A dollar and a half just to see 'em
    Don't it always seem to go
    That you don't know what you've got
    Till it's gone
    They paved paradise

---

[1] Joni Mitchell, in *Ladies of the Canyon* 1970 MCA records

And put up a parking lot.

*"Woodstock"*
We are stardust
We are golden
We are billion-year-old carbon
And we've got to get ourselves
Back to the garden

Both, in different ways, are harking back to a time when there was perfection, and lamenting the state we are in. "Woodstock" in particular was optimistic, believing we may be able to "get ourselves back to the garden". It was composed after the famous Woodstock festival, the high water mark of hippy hope in 1969. Yet later in the same year came the Altamont festival in San Francisco where violence broke out and the ideals of the hippy movement came crashing down. I think it is fair to say that there has never been such optimism since that time, certainly among the young. For it is not possible to "get ourselves back to the garden". The normal state of humanity is to "pave over paradise". Our longings to return to the glories and joys of Eden are just that: fruitless longings. Until we come to the temple.

Here we have God's pattern to bring us back into a right relationship with him. The temple he ordained was designed, literally, to bring his people back to the Garden. The carvings may be wooden and the lampstand only an imitation tree of life, but that is the intention. The people could return to their relationship with God by entering this garden-like temple, where God dwelt in his glory as he had done in Eden. The great difference between Eden and the later temples is sacrifice. In Eden there is no need for a sacrifice; in the temple there is, to purify the worshippers as they come to God.

And so today, if I am a temple of the Holy Spirit, if we are the temple of the Holy Spirit, and if Jesus is the temple raised again, where is the sacrifice? The answer is that Jesus was both the temple *and* the sacrifice. He is the sacrifice that allows us back to the Garden. As we trust in his work on the cross, we come into the presence of God. There is no longer a need for a temple because *the* sacrifice has happened.

Yet it is not the end of the story. We are manifestly not back in Eden. We are in a relationship with God, but it is still impaired. We still fall and need to repent. We increasingly understand the desires of God in care for nature, but our work for a better care is too little, too late. We try to do God's will in, for example, buying Fair Trade, and so working for justice. However we find injustice, often through ourselves, grows. We get glimpses of Eden, we taste the fruit of the tree of life, we know the presence of God with us, but it seems never for long, and never enough. We still await the final consummation.

That lies in the final "temple", the one where the Lord and Lamb are the temple in the heavenly Jerusalem. Here the image does include trees of life around the river of life, but it also includes the buildings of the city. Both the City and the Garden are images of the same thing: a perfect state where we can dwell forever in the presence of God. In that place there is healing of the nations, a removal of the curse, and the light of God.

Those Byzantines who made the mosaics in the Omayyad Mosque had it exactly right. They not only depicted vegetation, cultivation and rivers; they also showed towns, houses and palaces. Their vision was of the Garden and the City becoming one in the place of God. Sadly, their work was for a faith that had conquered theirs, but they still found a way to testify. Yet even if those mosaics had been in a church, they would still have been no more than a visual aid. We cannot get back to the Garden, but we can know God. And we can look forward to a time when the Garden will be renewed, God will walk in it, and we, like Adam and Eve of old, will know no pain.

**Questions to consider:**
    How can we walk with God in the Garden now?
    What will that walk be like when we are in the garden/city to
    come?

# 3. The Covenant

*Genesis 28:10-19*

[10]*Jacob left Beersheba and set out for Haran.* [11]*When he reached a certain place, he stopped for the night because the sun had set. Taking one of the stones there, he put it under his head and lay down to sleep.* [12]*He had a dream in which he saw a stairway resting on the earth, with its top reaching to heaven, and the angels of God were ascending and descending on it.* [13]*There above it stood the* LORD, *and he said: "I am the* LORD, *the God of your father Abraham and the God of Isaac. I will give you and your descendants the land on which you are lying.* [14]*Your descendants will be like the dust of the earth, and you will spread out to the west and to the east, to the north and to the south. All peoples on earth will be blessed through you and your offspring.* [15]*I am with you and will watch over you wherever you go, and I will bring you back to this land. I will not leave you until I have done what I have promised you."* [16]*When Jacob awoke from his sleep, he thought, "Surely the* LORD *is in this place, and I was not aware of it."* [17]*He was afraid and said, "How awesome is this place! This is none other than the house of God; this is the gate of heaven."* [18]*Early the next morning Jacob took the stone he had placed under his head and set it up as a pillar and poured oil on top of it.* [19]*He called that place Bethel (which means the house of God).*

*Hebrews 11:8-10*

[8]*By faith Abraham, when called to go to a place he would later receive as his inheritance, obeyed and went, even though he did not know where he was going.* [9]*By faith he made his home in the promised land like a stranger in a foreign country; he lived in tents, as did Isaac and Jacob, who were heirs with him of the same promise.* [10]*For he was looking forward to the city with foundations, whose architect and builder is God.*

There was nothing to see from horizon to horizon. In the middle of the Jordanian desert there was only dull brown sand, slight undulations, a few outcrops of rock and some scattered pebbles and boulders. In one or two dried watercourses a thorny shrub struggled for life. Yet at my feet there was a pile of stones, about three feet high. They were collected together and deliberately placed by human hand. Why? They were a boundary marker, though in such barrenness it was hard to see a purpose. Yet there they were.

At Bethel, Jacob set up such a marker, although it was more than just a boundary marker. It was a marker of the presence of God, and it was an altar. By pouring oil on the stone Jacob set it apart like an altar.

This story has been a Sunday school favourite for generations, with pictures of angels going up and down the ladder. Yet it is also a very serious staging post in God's dealing with humankind, including the establishment of the temple. The clue lies in Jacob's exclamation, that "this is none other than the house of God". On the face of it, it is a bizarre statement. There were no walls, no roof, no sanctuary. Yet, for Jacob, this was God's house, because it was the place where God dwelt and where he met him.

It was not the first time, nor the last, for an altar to be built at Bethel. In Genesis 12:8 Abraham is in the hills east of Bethel, having just met the Lord, and he builds an altar and pitches his tent. In Genesis 35 God appears to Jacob again at Bethel, and he sets up a pillar of stone as an altar.

There is another theme running through these stories, and that is the covenant promises of God. On each of these occasions God makes his solemn covenant to the Patriarchs. It also occurs in Genesis 17, Genesis 22 and twice in Genesis 26; the first two to Abraham, the second two to Isaac. In Genesis 17 the covenant is followed by the institution of circumcision. The first occasion in Genesis 26 is the only one not in the Promised Land. On every other occasion (Genesis 12, 22, 26, 28 and 35) when God appears and gives his covenant, the patriarchs respond by setting up an altar, usually on a hill (either Bethel or Mount. Moriah, where Solomon's temple was eventually built) in the territory God promised. The one other case was Beersheba, the border of the Promised Land.

The covenant promise, on each occasion, can be summed up as follows: the blessing of God; the promise and command for fruitfulness; the promise to fill and subdue the land (of Canaan); the promise to rule over the land. The building of altars where God appeared acted as a setting up of boundary markers, or the planting of flags saying, "This is now the place of the one true God." It is rather like an occupying power gradually invading an alien territory. God, through his covenant people, gradually extended the territory of his kingdom. Something similar happened when the allies invaded Iraq, and this and other invasions generally bring a negative image to our minds: who gave the invading force the right? However a better picture is that of the allies in World War 2 gradually pushing back the occupation of the Nazi forces: true justice and ownership was being restored. God's covenant begins with the true purpose for humankind.

As we continue with the story of the temple and the covenant promises we see that God was not merely establishing a piece of real estate where his people could live. It may appear so at first sight, but the context of the whole Bible is illuminating. The very first covenant from God to humankind is in Genesis. "God blessed them and said to them, "Be fruitful and increase in number; fill the earth and subdue it. Rule over the fish of the sea and the birds of the air and over every living creature that moves on the ground (Genesis 1:28)." Thus first humans are blessed, commanded to be fruitful, to subdue the whole earth and to rule over every living thing. Similarly the Patriarchs are blessed, promised fruitfulness, given the land of Canaan (but not the whole earth) and authority over it, and built these forerunners of the temple, Bethel. On at least two other occasions the temple is connected to the covenant. In Exodus 24 and 25 God appears to Moses and the elders of Israel on Mount Sinai and confirms the covenant. He then commands the making of the tabernacle. Similarly, when the temple is built by Solomon on Mount Moriah, God says, "If you or your sons turn away from me

and do not observe the commands and decrees I have given you…
then I will cut Israel off from the land I have given them and I will
reject this temple I have consecrated for my name" (1 Kings 9:6-7).
The covenant and the temple are inextricably linked and are seen to
be conditional upon the faithfulness of God's people. They did, in
due course, fail, and the temple was destroyed.

The covenant and temple are then linked by Jesus. "This is my
blood of the new covenant" he tells his disciples, shortly before
fulfilling his prophecy that the temple will be rebuilt in three days.
Jesus gave similar promises to his disciples as God had done in
the earlier covenants: they are blessed by him, told to be fruitful
in mission, told to pray for the coming of the kingdom of God,
promised to be rulers alongside Christ, and promised a renewed
heaven and earth.

The original promise in the Garden of Eden is renewed in full by
Jesus. We can follow each step along the way. The covenant is first
made, then re-established by God in more limited terms, and then
renewed by Jesus back to its fullness of territory (the whole earth)
and mission (all creation). And at each point worship of God in the
temple is essential.

God's message to humankind is that he is faithful, and that
his covenant is broad and wonderful. The covenant promises of
God naturally lead to worship because they display the greatness
of God. We read in Hebrews that "Abraham was looking forward
to the city with foundations, whose architect and builder is God".
Even the Patriarchs knew that the promises were not limited to the
simple human desire to expand and conquer, even for the extension
of God's rule.

It is at this point that we come to the conundrum of the here
and now. The promise to the Patriarchs only involved the land of
Canaan and their physical descendants, but was merely the shadow
of the real thing. This has implications for today. How are we, as
God's covenant people, to worship God today?

Let me give an example of where Christians went wrong.
You may remember the West End show, "Jerry Springer: the
Opera" which ran in London from 2003. There were widespread
complaints by Christians that the show was blasphemous (as indeed

it is). There were demonstrations, threats and abuse by Christians against the BBC and those involved in the play. How should we react? It comes to the heart of the question of the covenant and the temple. I have little doubt that the show grieved God's heart. It may have been clever, even a morality play, but the means it used was unacceptable. As covenantal believers, we are right to be saddened that God's way is so ignored. But as those worshipping the God of Abraham, Isaac and Jacob, as revealed in Jesus, how should we respond? It is unChrist-like to stand up for God in an aggressive or discourteous way. It was shocking to hear some of the insulting words by Christians on the radio. The new covenant revealed by Jesus shows that our worship of him demands the carrying of the cross. It demands that we do not fight persecution, but love our persecutor. It demands, *as our spiritual worship*, that we oppose evil using the weapons of Jesus: love, sacrifice and dependence on God. "Blessed are you when people insult you, persecute you and falsely say all kinds of evil against you because of me. Rejoice and be glad, for great is your reward in heaven…" But woe betide us if people can truthfully say all kinds of evil against us. Where then is our worship of our great God in the temple?

When Jacob met with God, received the promises, set up his stone and called the place Bethel he was part of the unique way God dealt with his world. We are now the inheritors of God's love and mercy through Christ. If today we have met with God, and know the depth of his promises, we too can worship at Bethel, the house of God.

## Questions to consider

How has Jesus fulfilled the covenant given to the Patriarchs?
What is true worship when we see the commands of God broken?

# 4. A Temple made with Hands?

*1 Kings 8:1, 3, 6, 10-13, 22, 27-29*

*[After the temple had been completed]* ¹*King Solomon summoned into his presence at Jerusalem the elders of Israel, ...* ³*When all the elders of Israel had arrived, the priests took up the ark...* ⁶ *(and) brought the ark of the LORD's covenant to its place in the inner sanctuary of the temple, the Most Holy Place, and put it beneath the wings of the cherubim...* ¹⁰*When the priests withdrew from the Holy Place, the cloud filled the temple of the LORD.* ¹¹*And the priests could not perform their service because of the cloud, for the glory of the LORD filled his temple.* ¹²*Then Solomon said, "The LORD has said that he would dwell in a dark cloud;* ¹³*I have indeed built a magnificent temple for you, a place for you to dwell for ever."...* ²²*Then Solomon stood before the altar of the LORD in front of the whole assembly of Israel, spread out his hands towards heaven* ²³*and said...* ²⁷*"But will God really dwell on earth? The heavens, even the highest heaven, cannot contain you. How much less this temple I have built!* ²⁸*Yet give attention to your servant's prayer and his plea for mercy, O LORD my God. Hear the cry and the prayer that your servant is praying in your presence this day.* ²⁹*May your eyes be open towards this temple night and day, this place of which you said, 'My Name shall be there,' so that you will hear the prayer your servant prays towards this place".*

*Acts 7:44-57*

*[Stephen said,]* ⁴⁴*"Our forefathers had the tabernacle of the Testimony with them in the desert. It had been made as God directed Moses, according to the pattern he had seen.* ⁴⁵*Having received the tabernacle... it remained in the land until the time of David.* ⁴⁷*But it was Solomon who built the house for him.* ⁴⁸*"However, the Most High does not live in houses made*

*by men. As the prophet says:* [49] *'Heaven is my throne, and the earth is my footstool. What kind of house will you build for me? says the Lord. Or where will my resting place be?* [50] *Has not my hand made all these things?'* [51] *You stiff–necked people, with uncircumcised hearts and ears! You are just like your fathers: You always resist the Holy Spirit!* [52] *Was there ever a prophet your fathers did not persecute? They even killed those who predicted the coming of the Righteous One. And now you have betrayed and murdered him—* [53]*you who have received the law that was put into effect through angels but have not obeyed it."* [54]*When they heard this, they were furious and gnashed their teeth at him.* [55]*But Stephen, full of the Holy Spirit, looked up to heaven and saw the glory of God, and Jesus standing at the right hand of God.* [56] *"Look,"* he said, "I see heaven open and the Son of Man standing at the right hand of God."* [57]*At this (they stoned him).*

The oldest Protestant church in Beirut is Presbyterian. It was built when the first American missionaries came and is in one of the most prominent positions in the centre of town. In the terrible Lebanese civil war (1975-1990) it was on the green line between the warring parties and was almost completely destroyed. After the war finished the congregation had a great rebuilding project. The outside of the building is as close as possible a replica of the original, although there is updating in the interior. What made the community rebuild the church, at great expense, in the same way? Why didn't they sell the highly valuable land, and build elsewhere with greater finance available? The answer lies in a shared memory, an honouring of the past when God worked, an honouring of God for his faithfulness. That church is now thriving.

The temple of Solomon replaced the tabernacle, and was itself rebuilt twice, on the same site, until it was finally destroyed in AD 70. The great temple of Solomon was built exactly as God directed, on the site where he had met Abraham. When it was dedicated the glory of God came to the temple in a dark cloud. Solomon claimed, with understandable if foolish pride, that he had built a magnificent temple, a place for God to dwell forever. Yet in almost the next breath, in his prayer, he knows that his temple cannot contain God. Even the heavens cannot do that. God came because he promised, not because human beings could cage him.

And so we come to one of the great tensions to do with the temple: the promise from God to dwell in the temple, and the inability for the temple ever to be great enough. The resolution to this, as we have already seen in brief, is to see the Garden of Eden/the heavenly City of Jerusalem as the true temple (because God dwells there, and there is no building), and anything else as temporary institutions. Yet there is a great human desire to cling to the physical, the truth contained in bricks and mortar, especially when it represents the presence of God in the past.

The speech of Stephen in Acts 7 is long and often passed over for the exciting climax where he sees Jesus and is stoned to death. One great emphasis of his speech is the temple. Stephen's speech, although lengthy, gives carefully edited highlights of the history of God's people. It ends, perhaps surprisingly for us, with the temple. Stephen's primary accusation against the Jewish leaders is their misunderstanding about the temple. "The Most High does not live in houses made by men" he says. He then accuses them of having uncircumcised hearts (in short, they are only Jews outwardly) and that they have resisted the Holy Spirit. This is strong stuff! It is only then that he says they did not recognise the Messiah in their midst, and that they murdered him.

Their rage is not only because he accused them of murder. It is because he declared them, and their temple, illegitimate. It is compounded by what happens next. He says he sees heaven open with Jesus standing at the right hand of God, who was there in all his glory. Where is it that they thought God dwelt? The answer is in the Holy of Holies in the temple in Jerusalem, in whose shadow Stephen spoke. It was in the Most Holy Place that the glory had first descended in Solomon's temple. Stephen does not need the temple to experience God, nor to be justified before him. He sees God and Jesus in the heavenly Jerusalem. Stephen is stoned to death for blasphemy, the blasphemy of undermining the temple. Jesus had done the same, and had met a similar end.

The great doctrine is this: the Most High does not live in houses built by men. Stephen had quoted Isaiah 66:1-2 in his inflammatory speech. God says there, "Has not *my* hand made all these things?" This is very close to the accusation made against Jesus by the false witnesses before the High Priest in Mark 14:58. He is claimed to have said, "I will destroy this temple made with hands, and three days I will build another made without hands." In John 2 Jesus does not use these exact words; he does claim that if they destroy the temple he will raise it again in three days (John 2:19). The issue is one of the most sensitive in Jerusalem: is the temple made "by hands" or through the will of God?

Hebrews 9:11 speaks of the risen Jesus entering a "greater and more perfect tabernacle that is not man-made, that is to say, not part of this creation." Paul also says that God does not live in temples made with hands (Acts 17:24). The implication is that "a temple made with hands" is the place for idols. New believers have a house not made with hands (2 Corinthians 5:1) whilst non-believing Jews are circumcised by hand (Ephesians 2:11). This relates back not only to Isaiah 66, but another passage essential in our study of the temple, Daniel 2:34. "A rock was cut out, but not by human hands."

Work with human hands is considered idolatrous when it comes to the things of God. Stephen himself, in Acts 7:41, says the golden calf was made with hands. Are then the original tabernacle and temple idolatrous? They are only if they did not follow God's express wishes (as happened with the golden calf). Rather, there was a contract between God and his people. If they fulfilled his commands, he would be with them in the temple. When they rebelled, the glory left and the temple was destroyed. The temple had become an idol itself. This is what was happening in the time of Jesus, but they did not have the insight to realise it. The power, prestige and authority of the ruling elite were bound up in the temple. The first Christians used the temple for worship, but only temporarily.

The destruction of the temple this time would be permanent, because it had been replaced by a temple not made with hands. It is Jesus who is the temple for us today, and in his resurrection he had destroyed the need for a "hand-made" temple forever. When the temple was finally destroyed in AD 70, it caused a crisis for Judaism. How could the Jewish religion function without sacrifice in Jerusalem and pilgrimage to Jerusalem? A new Judaism emerged which became known as Christianity. Christians weathered the storm over the temple destruction without any problem at all. They had no need of sacrifice or a Holy of Holies, or a priestly cast. They had Jesus.

Where does this leave us today? The answer, happily, is in the same place as those early Christians. For us, as for them, buildings are not essential. They should be functional. They can be beautiful. If intended as a place of worship, they should have aids to encourage worship: musical instruments, for example, and Bibles. But they are not essential. When persecution comes, the first things to go are the buildings. Churches may have been built following the leading of God. They may have been set apart, consecrated for use. They may have seen times of great glory, when the Spirit of God moved in power. But in the last analysis, they are expendable, because of Jesus. Our temple is Jesus, and the living stones that make up his body. If even the great temple, where God had promised to live, has been replaced, we must take great care not to elevate our church buildings to the same position.

Was the Presbyterian Church in Beirut wrong to rebuild their church in such a way? I do not believe so, because it was intended as a witness. It is today a testimony to the faithfulness of God during the war, and a testimony that such violence must not succeed. There is a place for great buildings. However if the elders, or the congregation, or the minister, begin to look towards the building rather than the Lord, then all the work of rebuilding will have been in vain. Worse, they would have created an idol.

All of us today need to beware of slipping into the trap of regarding our buildings above their station. It was a primary cause of the crucifixion of Jesus. He died, at least in part, because people regarded their building too highly. We can do the same, and it will also lead to the death of Christ in our hearts and in our community. And it is not only those with buildings who must beware. There are some Christians who do not meet in a purpose-built church who regard this with great pride. Their building is not "hand-made", but in their hearts it might as well be.

We are the followers of Jesus, who have in him all we need, with building or without. We must look to him for the pattern of our worship.

## Questions to consider

How do you view your church building?

How much time and money is spent on it, compared to following Jesus?

What is he saying about your use of the building?

# 5. Incense

*Exodus 30:1-9, 34-38*

[1]*"Make an altar of acacia wood for burning incense.* [2]*It is to be square, a cubit long and a cubit wide, and two cubits high—its horns of one piece with it.* [3]*Overlay the top and all the sides and the horns with pure gold, and make a gold moulding around it.* [4]*Make two gold rings for the altar below the moulding—two on opposite sides—to hold the poles used to carry it.* [5]*Make the poles of acacia wood and overlay them with gold.* [6]*Put the altar in front of the curtain that is before the ark of the Testimony—before the atonement cover that is over the Testimony—where I will meet with you.* [7]*Aaron must burn fragrant incense on the altar every morning when he tends the lamps.* [8]*He must burn incense again when he lights the lamps at twilight so that incense will burn regularly before the LORD for the generations to come.* [9]*Do not offer on this altar any other incense or any burnt offering or grain offering, and do not pour a drink offering on it…"* [34]*Then the LORD said to Moses, "Take fragrant spices—gum resin, onycha and galbanum—and pure frankincense, all in equal amounts,* [35]*and make a fragrant blend of incense, the work of a perfumer. It is to be salted and pure and sacred.* [36]*Grind some of it to powder and place it in front of the Testimony in the Tent of Meeting, where I will meet with you. It shall be most holy to you.* [37]*Do not make any incense with this formula for yourselves; consider it holy to the LORD.* [38]*Whoever makes any like it to enjoy its fragrance must be cut off from his people."*

*Jeremiah 1:16*

[16]*I will pronounce my judgments on my people because of their wickedness in forsaking me, in burning incense to other gods and in worshipping what their hands have made.*

*Revelation 5:8*
> [8]*And when he had taken it, the four living creatures and the twenty-four elders fell down before the Lamb. Each one had a harp and they were holding golden bowls full of incense, which are the prayers of the saints.*

*Matthew 2:11*
> [11]*On coming to the house, they saw the child with his mother Mary, and they bowed down and worshipped him. Then they opened their treasures and presented him with gifts of gold and of incense and of myrrh.*

The next few chapters take a closer look at the activities in the tabernacle (and by extension much of the activities in the later temples) as described in Exodus and Leviticus.

In the western world incense has seen a remarkable increase in popularity in the last few decades. Much of this is linked to a fascination with eastern religions and the sale of joss sticks in the 1960's. However for very many centuries incense has been used in Christian worship.

A little while ago I attended the induction of an Anglican vicar in his church. The church is of the Anglo-Catholic persuasion and the use of incense was extensive. The censer, containing the incense, was used during the entrance procession and then swung vigorously over the altar before the service began. When it came to the reading of the gospel, the bible was paraded down the centre of the aisle and liberally censed. By now, as you imagine, there were thick clouds of incense throughout the church. It did not end there. When the bread and wine were brought up the censer was swung over them; the ministers and the people then had incense swung over them. Finally at the Holy Communion the cup and bread were lifted high and censed with abandon. The church, and particularly the area around the communion table, resembled a thick fog.

Why? What was the point? How does this help our worship

of God? We go all the way back to Exodus to find God's original command to use incense in the tabernacle. In the tabernacle there was to be a special altar for burning incense, in front of the curtain which hid the Ark of the Covenant in the Most Holy Place. God specifically tells Moses that it is to be burned before the very place "where I will meet with you." (Exodus 30:6) Aaron is commanded to burn incense in the morning and evening so that it will burn regularly, and it is to be burned for generations to come.

The command does not tell us why it is to be burned; only that it is an essential element of worship of God, in his presence in the tabernacle and later in the temple. It is known that in the ancient world incense was burned for a variety of reasons. It could be used simply to give a pleasant perfume in the house (in the same way we would use air freshener, although it was a remarkably expensive air freshener!). It was also used for processions and festivities. However most of the uses were religious—as a sacrifice to the pagan gods; to drive away evil spirits; or as a means of purification. The ancient Israelites were by no means alone in using incense. The trade in incense was essential and extremely lucrative.

Frankincense in the ancient world came from only one region, the area around the Horn of Africa. It could only be found in modern day Yemen and parts of modern Oman and Saudi Arabia, and across the sea in Somalia. These kingdoms included Sheba of old, the land of the Queen of Sheba. Arabia Felix was the Roman name for the south-west of Arabia. It means "happy Arabia" in part because the area enjoyed higher rainfall and was therefore fertile and productive but also because the peculiar geography of hills, precipitation and thin soils enabled it to grow the trees that produced frankincense and myrrh. According to Herodotus (5th century BC), "In it [Arabia] alone of all lands grow frankincense and myrrh and cassia and cinnamon."[1]. The expense of incense was not only due to the monopoly one area had on production, it was also due to the expense of transport. The main trade route to the Mediterranean area led through the deserts of Arabia by camel train, and as such it became proverbial:

*"Who is this coming up from the desert like a column of smoke,*

---

[1] *The History of Herodotus*, Book 3 paragraph 107; trans. G. C. Macaulay, Barnes and Noble, 2004

*perfumed with myrrh and incense*
*made from all the spices of the merchant?*
*Look! It is Solomon's carriage." Song of Songs 3:6*

Exodus suggests a special purpose for this incense in the tabernacle, above and beyond the normal uses of incense. It was a sacrifice to the Lord Almighty because it was offered at the altar and it was extremely costly. And looking at Exodus 30:34-38, we know it was a special incense. There is a precise recipe for this incense and there was a severe punishment if anyone used this incense for another purpose: they were to be cut off from the people. The incense was holy, set apart for a special purpose.

This reinforces the primary reason for its usage: to symbolise the presence of God. It was intended to be a God-ordained memorial of himself as he appeared to Moses in the smoke on Mount Sinai and in the tabernacle. Exodus 19:18 describes Moses meeting with God like this, "Mount Sinai was covered with smoke, because the Lord descended on it in fire. The smoke billowed up from it like smoke from a furnace…" Again in Exodus 40:34-35 we read, "Then the cloud covered the Tent of Meeting, and the glory of the Lord filled the tabernacle. Moses could not enter the Tent of Meeting because the cloud had settled upon it, and the glory of the Lord had filled the tabernacle."

It is difficult for us in the twenty-first century to realise what the clouds of incense would have felt like to the people in the tabernacle. Today we live in a world which is easily sensual. The sounds and visions on a computer or T.V. screen are everywhere. Our senses are bombarded daily so that we are desensitised. Back then the incense would have been overwhelming: the sight and the smells rare and wonderful and combined with an overwhelming desire to worship God as he deserved. Even today incense in a church can be impressive if we are not used to it. Then it would have been overwhelming, a direct reminder of the presence of God.

The glory of the Lord was in the mysterious cloud and the cloud of incense represented this. This is the context for the use of incense in the church described earlier. Incense was used whenever God was deemed to be especially present: among his people, in his holy word, and in the bread and wine.

However it has to be said that incense, which has been popular in Eastern and Roman churches for many centuries, was not greatly used in the first three centuries of the Christian faith. At that time incense was used in pagan worship throughout the Roman world and Christians thought it better not to be associated with that. Only later, when Christianity became the established religion of the Empire did it start to be used more widely, when it could no longer be associated with idols. The example from Jeremiah 1 is typical of how incense could be abused. It could be burned to other gods as well as the Lord God and was perhaps the deepest sign of apostasy by his people in the Old Testament. Like all good things it could be abused as well as used for a godly purpose.

There is another meaning that is often associated with incense, and that is prayer. There are surprisingly few references in the Bible to this given the popularity of the idea. There are three principle texts. Psalm 141:2 and Revelation 8:3 compare prayer rising to God like incense rises to God. Revelation 5:8 is the only verse that says directly that prayer is incense and this verse is clearly symbolic. Prayer is not incense and incense is not prayer but image of incense rising to God is useful in inspiring prayer.

After the Reformation incense virtually ceased in Protestant churches. It was seen (along with other sensual aspects to worship) to be superstitious and detracting from the faith. Incense was no longer aiding worship of God but taking people from a true understanding of him. Today (at least in the West) a different culture prevails. In a postmodern world incense is seen to be spiritual and mystical and may indeed once more help people worship God. However at the same time in postmodernity symbols are being emptied of their agreed content; thus incense may also confuse true worship. The same ambiguous nature of worship seen in the Old Testament can still be traced today.

So how can incense help us to live in God's presence today? Is it necessary to burn copious quantities of incense as my neighbouring church did? Is the symbol still valid? Does God still expect it? In order to answer these questions we need to return to Jesus. Many

Old Testament commands are fulfilled by him and in him. This is particularly true of the commands concerning worship of the Lord God in the tabernacle/temple. Regarding incense however there is only one slender hint: the gifts of the Magi to the new-born Jesus. The gifts included frankincense and traditionally this has always been seen as a symbol of the status of the new-born Messiah himself rather than something Mary and Joseph were to burn themselves in the temple. Gold for a king; myrrh for a death; but incense for glory. In some way the glory of the eternal God had come to earth in the form of a baby, and the Magi from the east recognised this.

Incense is no longer necessary but it can be useful. More important than the specifics of incense is how we can learn to connect with the glory and mystery of God as those Israelites were commanded to do long ago.

## Questions to consider

Should you use incense in your church?

How can we connect with the glory and mystery of God in worship today?

# 6. The Census and the Atonement Money

*Exodus 30:11-16*

[11]*Then the L*ORD *said to Moses,* [12]*"When you take a census of the Israelites to count them, each one must pay the L*ORD *a ransom for his life at the time he is counted. Then no plague will come on them when you number them.* [13]*Each one who crosses over to those already counted is to give a half shekel, according to the sanctuary shekel, which weighs twenty gerahs. This half shekel is an offering to the L*ORD*.* [14]*All who cross over, those twenty years old or more, are to give an offering to the L*ORD*.* [15]*The rich are not to give more than a half shekel and the poor are not to give less when you make the offering to the L*ORD *to atone for your lives.* [16]*Receive the atonement money from the Israelites and use it for the service of the Tent of Meeting. It will be a memorial for the Israelites before the L*ORD*, making atonement for your lives."*

*Hebrews 10:19-31*

[19]*Therefore, brothers, since we have confidence to enter the Most Holy Place by the blood of Jesus,* [20]*by a new and living way opened for us through the curtain, that is, his body,* [21]*and since we have a great priest over the house of God,* [22]*let us draw near to God with a sincere heart in full assurance of faith, having our hearts sprinkled to cleanse us from a guilty conscience and having our bodies washed with pure water.* [23]*Let us hold unswervingly to the hope we profess, for he who promised is faithful.* [24]*And let us consider how we may spur one another on towards love and good deeds.* [25]*Let us not give up meeting together, as some are in the habit of doing, but let us encourage one another—and all the more as you see the Day approaching.* [26]*If we deliberately keep on sinning after we have received the knowledge of the truth, no sacrifice for sins is left,* [27]*but only a fearful expectation of judgment and of raging fire that will consume the enemies of God.*

*[28]Anyone who rejected the law of Moses died without mercy on the testimony of two or three witnesses. [29]How much more severely do you think a man deserves to be punished who has trampled the Son of God under foot, who has treated as an unholy thing the blood of the covenant that sanctified him, and who has insulted the Spirit of grace? [30]For we know him who said, "It is mine to avenge; I will repay," and again, "The Lord will judge his people." [31]It is a dreadful thing to fall into the hands of the living God.*

Each week in church we have the collection. The side's people stand at the end of the rows, as is right and proper. The congregation shuffles a little and reaches for their money. Some visitors feel a little affronted and look for a small coin, whilst others are generous. Many of the regulars simply pass the bag, mystifying to an outsider, until it is explained that they may be already paying by standing order. The collection bags are then put together and solemnly brought up to the front on a plate to the minister, who prays that the gifts may be used for the glory of God. Something like that happens in churches all over the world, with regional variations. Solemnity may give way to dance and ushers to people moving purposely to the front, but the essence is the same. Money is collected. However we can go further, into the backstage of church life. Somewhere, sometime, the treasurer (or deputy) will count the money, preferably (legally!) with a witness to check. And someone, somewhere, will count the congregation and put a number in a book. Often the minister will disagree, believing it to be higher! And both these figures, the money and people, will often be passed on to the higher authority that collects such statistics.

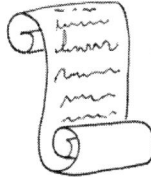

At least, that is what happens in my church, week in, week out! It appears similar in Exodus 30:11-16 at the tabernacle. It is somewhat comforting to know that there are such huge similarities in organised religion—we all need to do it! But Exodus gives us rather more. v.12: "When you take a census of the Israelites to count them, each one must pay…then no plague will come on them when you count them." What is that all about? I imagine that the per capita giving in church would go up substantially if people believed they would get the plague otherwise, but I also suspect that overall attendance might go down at the same time!

This is not the only place that a census is commanded in scripture. God commands a census of the Israelites in Numbers 1 and Numbers 26. The first census is of the original generation that left Egypt; the second is the generation about to enter the Promised Land after 40 years of rebellion and punishment by God which included, among other things, plague.

Here is the key to why taking the census is such a dangerous procedure. In such a census we are counted unambiguously as belonging to God, with all the privileges and demands that brings. If we are part of God's people we need to know what that means. In reality therefore this census is less like counting numbers in church and more like reading entries in the baptism book (or confirmation book, depending on denomination). Those who have been "counted" as part of God's people have made their own profession or statement.

The method of counting commanded by God in Exodus was dramatic. It was only for adult (20 years old and over) males. They needed to cross over from one side to the other for the census to take place to avoid the possibility of double counting (perhaps a system that could be adopted in church?!). One can imagine the scene in the desert in front of the tabernacle as the number gradually dwindled until finally there was only a small group left, and then only one. This was no mere counting of heads; it was a holy procedure saying, "I am on the Lord's side." Perhaps we really could adopt this procedure in church, not as a way of helping rather harassed sides people, but rather as a way of reaffirming commitment.

Hebrews 10 shows us how this works out after Jesus. The blood of Jesus in the ultimate atonement means we have access not only to the tabernacle courtyard but into the Most Holy Place itself. We have access to God the Father in all his majesty. But rather more disturbing (and giving lie to the idea that there is no judgement by God in the New Testament) is the punishment for "keeping on sinning". "If we deliberately keep on sinning after we have received the knowledge of the truth, no sacrifice for sins is left, but only a fearful expectation of judgment." This is one of the most difficult verses in the New Testament but it finds context in the events in the book of Exodus. Keeping on sinning, in this context, means total apostasy, not just doing some things wrong (which every Christian does). It means a complete, deliberate turning away from God and all he has done in Jesus. Moreover it is not referring to someone who "slips away from the faith" in (for example) depression or disillusionment from the church. There may be a judgement for that but it is not the judgement referred to here. This judgement is for those who rebel against God whilst knowing his power their midst.

The writer to the Hebrews is clearly looking back to the events in the desert and the most obvious one is that of the worship of the Golden Calf. Moses had gone to the mountain, as commanded, and the people lost heart and faith. They had recent, extensive experience of the grace of God in both miraculous deliverance from the Egyptians and miraculous provision of food and yet they turned to worship another God. This is the "keep on sinning" referred to in Hebrews. Exodus 32:35 links with reference to plague in Exodus 30, "And the Lord struck the people with a plague because of what they did with the calf Aaron had made."

Hebrews may not be referring to any old sin but it is still intended as a serious warning, as is the census in Exodus 30. We can only come into God's presence knowing that we have no right to be there and knowing that we dare not turn to other gods. It is a dreadful thing to fall into the hands of the living God.

It is into this context that a financial payment is made. It wasn't simply the weekly offering, it was also an atonement offering; "Each one must pay the Lord a ransom for his life" (v.12). At first sight this seems to be a case of buying one's forgiveness, but there is more to it than that.

Everything in the worship in the tabernacle is in the context of the atonement sacrifice itself (see chapter 10). In comparison this is a minor ceremony. The whole point of the tabernacle was the centrality of the blood sacrifice (as we have seen, Jesus was the final, complete and great sacrifice). The payment of money is nothing compared to that. What is more, the amount of money paid is tiny, half a shekel. This "ransom" money is merely a token, a recognition that their lives were justly forfeit if they thought they could come before God in their own strength. Again there is the lesson for us: how do we come before the God?

This half shekel was as likely to be a weight as a coin. Half a shekel in weight was about 5.7 grams (0.2 of an ounce). The metal was probably silver and everyone, rich and poor, were to pay the same amount. It was a kind of a poll tax as well as atonement. It was kept low so that everyone could afford it and no-one was left out. It was an offering of thanksgiving, a love gift for the freedom given in the atonement and the crossing from one side to the other. The only real similarities with a church collection were that people gave freely and that it was used for the upkeep of the tabernacle.

The crossing from one side to the other as the payment is made is indicative of what happened at the Red Sea and (later) the River Jordan. It is a sign of what God has done and of what we have to do. In the Old Testament as much as today life in God cannot be inherited. His grace gives us the opportunity, but we still have to have the faith to respond. And we need to remain faithful and give back to him in gratitude a token of what he has done for us.

**Questions to consider**
How do you enter into God's presence for worship?
Do you come with a sense of being numbered as one of his?
Are you a grateful giver and as one who is determined not to worship other gods?

# 7. The Basin for Washing

*Exodus 30:17-21*

<sup></sup>17 *Then the* LORD *said to Moses,* 18 *"Make a bronze basin, with its bronze stand, for washing. Place it between the Tent of Meeting and the altar, and put water in it.* 19 *Aaron and his sons are to wash their hands and feet with water from it.* 20 *Whenever they enter the Tent of Meeting, they shall wash with water so that they will not die. Also, when they approach the altar to minister by presenting an offering made to the* LORD *by fire,* 21 *they shall wash their hands and feet so that they will not die. This is to be a lasting ordinance for Aaron and his descendants for the generations to come."*

*Exodus 29:4-7*

<sup></sup>4 *Then bring Aaron and his sons to the entrance to the Tent of Meeting and wash them with water.* 5 *Take the garments and dress Aaron with the tunic, the robe of the ephod, the ephod itself and the breastpiece. Fasten the ephod on him by its skilfully woven waistband.* 6 *Put the turban on his head and attach the sacred diadem to the turban.* 7 *Take the anointing oil and anoint him by pouring it on his head.*

*Exodus 38:8*

<sup></sup>8 *They made the bronze basin and its bronze stand from the mirrors of the women who served at the entrance to the Tent of Meeting.*

*John 13:6-11*

<sup></sup>6 *He came to Simon Peter, who said to him, "Lord, are you going to wash my feet?"*
<sup></sup>7 *Jesus replied, "You do not realise now what I am doing, but later you will understand."*
<sup></sup>8 *"No," said Peter, "you shall never wash my feet." Jesus answered, "Unless I wash you, you have no part with me."*

⁹*"Then, Lord," Simon Peter replied, "not just my feet but my hands and my head as well!"*

¹⁰*Jesus answered, "A person who has had a bath needs only to wash his feet; his whole body is clean. And you are clean, though not every one of you." ¹¹For he knew who was going to betray him, and that was why he said not every one was clean.*

*Ephesians 5:25-27*

²⁵*Husbands, love your wives, just as Christ loved the church and gave himself up for her ²⁶to make her holy, cleansing her by the washing with water through the word, ²⁷and to present her to himself as a radiant church, without stain or wrinkle or any other blemish, but holy and blameless.*

In the autumn of 2009 the Church of England (together with a number of other churches) came close to developing a whole new liturgical rite. And it may still come about. This was the time, as fears of the swine 'flu virus grew, that all Anglican churches were very strongly advised to use antiseptic hand gel at Holy Communion. Many catholic-orientated churches already had extensive rituals concerning the washing of hands with water; now it would have to include hand gel...Well, the swine 'flu threat receded and with it strict advice over hand gel. But it may well be, as diseases resistant to modern antibiotics become more and more prevalent, that in a few years this advice will have legal force and there will have to be a way of accommodating hand gel officially into our services of worship! It would not be new. Washing and cleanliness have long had an important role in worship.

The command in Exodus 30:17 is uncomplicated. Moses is instructed to make a basin for washing. The dimensions are unknown but it was to be made from bronze and filled with water. It was to be located in the courtyard between the sacrificial altar and the tent. There the priests (Aaron, his sons and their descendants) were to wash their hands and feet before they entered the tent. If they did not they would die. They were also to wash before making a sacrifice at the altar (the "fire" offering in verse 20 probably referred to all normal sacrifices).

A little more can be found in other neighbouring texts. Exodus 29:4-7 speaks about the consecration of the priests. In that ritual they are to be brought to the entrance of the Tent of Meeting (the tabernacle) and washed before being clothed and anointed with oil. The obvious assumption is that they were washed in the bronze basin that stood there.

In Exodus 38:8 we learn that the bronze for the basin didn't come from the main offering of the people but from the women who served at the entrance of the tabernacle. In the days before glass, mirrors were made of polished metal that gave a poor reflection back. It is a nice detail: rather than look at themselves in their bronze mirrors, the women sacrificed their looks for the worship of God.

Why was the construction of a basin for washing so important? First of all we know that washing is very important in different religions. Modern Judaism's rules on washing have developed from the Old Testament and the Talmud but in the absence of the temple there is no direct comparison with the Bronze basin in Exodus. Another religion with strict rules on washing before worship is Islam, where the worshipper has to wash both his hands and feet before entering the mosque, rather like the priests of Judaism. Interestingly on the Temple Mount in Jerusalem, which is now the site of the Al Aqsa Mosque and the Dome of the Rock, there is a site for ablutions not so far from where the Bronze Basin might have stood. Christianity has other important rituals concerning water, but no direct comparison for reasons that shall become obvious.

For God's priests at the time of the book of Exodus living in the presence of God in the tabernacle required cleanliness. If they entered without washing they would die. There was an initial washing all over at their consecration and on every subsequent occasion they entered the tabernacle they had to wash their extremities. It is immediately apparent that there is a reference by Jesus concerning this.

At the last supper Jesus washes the disciples feet (perhaps in itself an echo of Exodus) and Peter objects. Jesus says that unless he washes Peter's feet Peter can have no part with him, to which Peter responds, impetuously and devotedly, that Jesus should wash him all over. And Jesus responds that it is not necessary because they are already clean.

The parallels with the priests in the Exodus account are very strong, especially when we read Peter's own teaching that the followers of Jesus make up a "royal priesthood" (1 Peter 2:9). The disciples had needed to be washed all over and they had been, through Jesus (John 13:10). This was the washing of being born again, the washing of regeneration. When Jesus commanded his disciples to go and baptise he was giving an outward sign of the experience that is already true spiritually for all who follow Jesus. Yet Jesus also teaches that the washing of feet (by him) was still necessary. The washing of the feet was usually done in those days by a servant in the house because the feet would inevitably become dirty through walking around. However we know that Jesus is speaking spiritually, not just practically. Presumably this washing was necessary for the same reason that the priests in Exodus had to wash: to remove from them the pollution of the daily world when they entered the presence of God. The first disciples, like the priests of old, needed their feet washed when coming to God. Yet Christians no longer do this today (unlike, say, Muslims). Why?

In Acts 21:26 we find the apostle Paul going to the temple and purifying himself before approaching God. This purification certainly involved water and was a continuation of the tradition from Exodus. Yet we also know that Paul only did this as a witness to his fellow Jews; he did not believe it was necessary. Ephesians 5:25-27 gives us the clue. In Ephesians 5 Paul tells us that Jesus gave himself up for the church, cleansing her by the washing with water through the word. The word used here for washing in the Greek is laver, the same word used in the Greek Old Testament for the bronze basin in the tabernacle. This then is not the washing of baptism but the continual washing of the foot-washing. To be washed by the word can mean two things. It could mean being washed through the word Jesus spoke or it could mean being washed by Jesus, the Word of God himself. It is unhelpful to separate these too much. The Word made flesh uttered the words of salvation. Nevertheless it is probably right to concentrate on one kind of "word" in particular: the word of confession which leads to Jesus word of forgiveness. Jesus came so that we could be, and continue to be, in a right relationship with God. He washes us for our presentation before God through his word. As Hebrews 10:22 says: "Let us draw near to God with a sincere heart in full assurance of faith, having our hearts sprinkled to cleanse us from a guilty conscience and having our bodies washed with pure water."

## Questions to consider

What is the equivalent to "giving away our mirrors"?
Many churches have re-instituted a Maundy Thursday foot-washing ceremony. Is this helpful when we consider washing?
How in practice do you feel you can be cleansed by the word?

# 8. Anointing Oil

*Exodus 30:22-33*

²²*Then the* LORD *said to Moses,* ²³*"Take the following fine spices: 500 shekels of liquid myrrh, half as much (that is, 250 shekels) of fragrant cinnamon, 250 shekels of fragrant cane,* ²⁴*500 shekels of cassia—all according to the sanctuary shekel—and a hin of olive oil.* ²⁵*Make these into a sacred anointing oil, a fragrant blend, the work of a perfumer. It will be the sacred anointing oil.* ²⁶*Then use it to anoint the Tent of Meeting, the ark of the Testimony,* ²⁷*the table and all its articles, the lampstand and its accessories, the altar of incense,* ²⁸*the altar of burnt offering and all its utensils, and the basin with its stand.* ²⁹*You shall consecrate them so they will be most holy, and whatever touches them will be holy.* ³⁰*"Anoint Aaron and his sons and consecrate them so they may serve me as priests.* ³¹*Say to the Israelites, 'This is to be my sacred anointing oil for the generations to come.* ³²*Do not pour it on men's bodies and do not make any oil with the same formula. It is sacred, and you are to consider it sacred.* ³³*Whoever makes perfume like it and whoever puts it on anyone other than a priest must be cut off from his people.' "*

*2 Samuel 6:1-8*

*David again brought together out of Israel chosen men, thirty thousand in all.* ²*He and all his men set out from Baalah of Judah to bring up from there the ark of God, which is called by the Name, the name of the* LORD *Almighty, who is enthroned between the cherubim that are on the ark.* ³*They set the ark of God on a new cart and brought it from the house of Abinadab, which was on the hill. Uzzah and Ahio, sons of Abinadab, were guiding the new cart* ⁴*with the ark of God on it, and Ahio was walking in front of it.* ⁵*David and the whole house of Israel were celebrating with all their might before the* LORD, *with songs and with harps, lyres,* *tambourines, sistrums and cymbals.* <sup>6</sup>*When they came to the threshing-floor of Nacon, Uzzah reached out and took hold of the ark of God, because the oxen stumbled.* <sup>7</sup>*The LORD's anger burned against Uzzah because of his irreverent act; therefore God struck him down and he died there beside the ark of God.* <sup>8</sup>*Then David was angry because the LORD's wrath had broken out against Uzzah, and to this day that place is called Perez Uzzah.*

*Isaiah 61:1-3*

<sup>1</sup>*The Spirit of the Sovereign LORD is on me, because the LORD has anointed me to preach good news to the poor. He has sent me to bind up the broken-hearted, to proclaim freedom for the captives and release from darkness for the prisoners,* <sup>2</sup>*to proclaim the year of the LORD's favour and the day of vengeance of our God, to comfort all who mourn,* <sup>3</sup>*and provide for those who grieve in Zion— to bestow on them a crown of beauty instead of ashes, the oil of gladness instead of mourning, and a garment of praise instead of a spirit of despair.*

*Acts 4:25-27*

<sup>25</sup>*You spoke by the Holy Spirit through the mouth of your servant, our father David: " 'Why do the nations rage and the peoples plot in vain?* <sup>26</sup> *The kings of the earth take their stand and the rulers gather together against the Lord and against his Anointed One.'* <sup>27</sup>*Indeed Herod and Pontius Pilate met together with the Gentiles and the people of Israel in this city to conspire against your holy servant Jesus, whom you anointed.*

Living in Beirut in the 1990s meant frequent power cuts. The power generators and the electricity grid had not yet been repaired properly after the war and so there was only electricity for a limited number of hours in the day. Having a power cut at, say, seven o'clock in the evening brought great inconvenience. Naturally we lost light (there were candles ready). We also lost heating because, although the central heating was oil burning the starting mechanism was electric. The electric cooker and microwave were also lost. The biggest worry was over the freezer and fridge: would the power come back (or the generator kick in) before the food was ruined? And obviously we lost the entertainment of T.V. and video. (Today one would add the computer to the list but in Beirut the telephone lines controlling internet access were also extremely poor…)

Why mention this litany of woes? It is difficult in our culture to understand the importance of the olive in a biblical culture; perhaps the only equivalent is electricity. They could no more do without the olive than we can do without electricity. Olive oil provided light through oil lamps. Olive oil was essential for cooking. Olive wood was used for heat in fires and for building timber. It was also carved for decoration (and still is today). Oil was a food in itself. A simple but nourishing meal was to dip bread in oil rather as we spread butter on bread. Naturally there were also the olive fruits. The olive tree, and its products, was essential to life throughout the Mediterranean world.

For Moses and the Israelites in the desert on the Mediterranean fringe olive oil was an even more precious commodity. Oil could only be obtained by trade. Olive trees do not grow in the desert, nor could they move with a wandering people!

Exodus 30:22-33 begins with a characteristic command, "Yahweh said to Moses". In these descriptions of the tabernacle we are dealing all the time with divine command. On this occasion the divine command is amazing; essentially it is a recipe.

Take 1 gallon of Olive Oil
11 kg of Myrrh
11 kg of Cassia
5 ½ kg of Cinnamon
5 ½ kg of fragrant cane

and then give them to an expert perfumer (v.25) and blend them together.

Like many ancient recipes it is difficult to know exactly what is meant. Was the myrrh liquid? If so that would make the final result more liquid, but then why give a dry weight? Myrrh and cinnamon are substances we know well. Cassia is a little more difficult;

probably it is the inner bark of the cinnamon cassia tree. "Fragrant cane" has been variously translated and is quite obscure. With no serious evidence some have said it was cannabis! However it is much more likely that it is the tip of the sugar cane plant.

The result was not so much oil as a sticky, very fragrant, paste. It was to be used to anoint everything to do with the tabernacle: the tent itself, the Ark of the Covenant, the Table, the Lampstand (which burnt oil for fuel), the altars and the Bronze Basin. It was also used to anoint the priests (v.30) to consecrate them alongside these objects.

The oil and everything it touched was to "set apart" for God. That is to say it was made holy. Verse 32 is clear that this oil was not to be used for any other purpose. If it was abused in this way the person making it or using it was to be cut off from the people. This was the opposite of being made holy; it meant being cut off from God's holiness and his holy things and people.

We receive here an understanding of God and his holiness. He is set apart because he is holy by his very nature. For us or any object to enter his presence we too must be made holy, i.e. set apart. One part of this process is by being anointed exactly as he said. Obedience is a key attribute in entering his presence; disobedience is key in being separated.

One example of this is Uzzah (2 Samuel 6:6-8). Uzzah accidentally touched the Holy Ark of the Covenant without permission. The oxen pulling the cart containing the ark stumbled and he put out his hand to steady the Ark. God struck him down dead for presuming to handle such a holy thing. At this point most westerners are struck by the unfairness of the situation; surely he was only trying to save the Ark from damage? But he had no right; and in any case, it was no real accident. The incident only happened because enough care was not being taken in the first place. The holiness of God is not to be trifled with.

A second theme that is linked with anointing is the presence of God by his Holy Spirit. In 1 Samuel 10:10 it says that the Spirit of

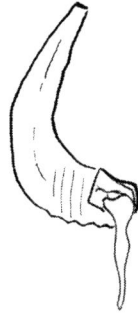

God came upon Saul after his anointing. Isaiah 61:1 says, "The Spirit of the Sovereign Lord is upon me, because he has anointed me..."

This is the same reference quoted by Jesus himself in the synagogue in Nazareth (Luke 4). He says that it applies to him; in other words he is an "anointed one".

This is not a one-off reference concerning Jesus. Jesus is anointed on his feet by the sinful woman (Luke 7:36). His dead body is anointed by the women (Mark 16:1). Following Palm Sunday the disciple's hopes that he is the Messiah are raised. Messiah literally means "the Anointed One" following references like Psalm 2. This conviction is confirmed following Jesus' resurrection. The disciple's prayer in Acts 4 refers to Jesus as the Anointed One (v.26 and 27). Peter, in his speech to Cornelius, says that "God anointed Jesus of Nazareth with the Holy Spirit and power" (Acts 10:38). Jesus is the standard of an anointed human being: filled with the Holy Spirit, anointed for a task that the Spirit empowered and, for those very reasons, set apart or made holy.

Just as Aaron and the priesthood were forerunners of Jesus, so Jesus' followers are also given the blessing of anointing. Paul tells us "he anointed us, set his seal of ownership on us, and put his Spirit in our hearts as a deposit, guaranteeing what is to come" (2 Corinthians 1:21-22). The anointing and the presence of the Holy Spirit upon people is limited in the Old Testament but God in his grace pours out the anointing of his Holy Spirit after Pentecost. The preserve of the priest, kings and prophets has been given to all the people of God. We too are holy, set apart, as the body of Christ and the temple of the Holy Spirit.

### Questions to consider

Is it helpful to be physically anointed today? Does this ever happen in your church?

Given some of the horrors in church history, how can we claim to be anointed? Does the glory of God still reside in his temple? If so, how?

# 9. Craftsmen in the Temple

*Exodus 31:1-11*

[1]*Then the LORD said to Moses,* [2] *"See I have chosen Bezalel son of Uri, the son of Hur, of the tribe of Judah,* [3]*and I have filled him with the Spirit of God, with skill, ability and knowledge in all kinds of crafts—* [4]*to make artistic designs for work in gold, silver and bronze,* [5]*to cut and set stones, to work in wood, and to engage in all kinds of craftsmanship.* [6]*Moreover, I have appointed Oholiab son of Ahisamach, of the tribe of Dan, to help him. Also I have given skill to all the craftsmen to make everything I have commanded you:* [7]*the Tent of Meeting, the ark of the Testimony with the atonement cover on it, and all the other furnishings of the tent—* [8]*the table and its articles, the pure gold lampstand and all its accessories, the altar of incense,* [9]*the altar of burnt offering and all its utensils, the basin with its stand—* [10]*and also the woven garments, both the sacred garments for Aaron the priest and the garments for his sons when they serve as priests,* [11]*and the anointing oil and fragrant incense for the Holy Place. They are to make them just as I commanded you."*

*2 Chronicles 3:4-7*

*(Solomon) overlaid the inside with pure gold.* [5]*He panelled the main hall with pine and covered it with fine gold and decorated it with palm tree and chain designs.* [6]*He adorned the temple with precious stones. And the gold he used was gold of Parvaim.* [7]*He overlaid the ceiling beams, door-frames, walls and doors of the temple with gold, and he carved cherubim on the walls.*

*2 Chronicles 7:16*

[16]*I have chosen and consecrated this temple so that my Name may be there for ever. My eyes and my heart will always be there.*

*John 12:1-8*

> ¹*Six days before the Passover, Jesus arrived at Bethany, where Lazarus lived, whom Jesus had raised from the dead.* ²*Here a dinner was given in Jesus' honour. Martha served, while Lazarus was among those reclining at the table with him.* ³*Then Mary took about a pint of pure nard, an expensive perfume; she poured it on Jesus' feet and wiped his feet with her hair. And the house was filled with the fragrance of the perfume.* ⁴*But one of his disciples, Judas Iscariot, who was later to betray him, objected,* ⁵*"Why wasn't this perfume sold and the money given to the poor? It was worth a year's wages."* ⁶*He did not say this because he cared about the poor but because he was a thief; as keeper of the money bag, he used to help himself to what was put into it.* ⁷*"Leave her alone," Jesus replied. "It was intended that she should save this perfume for the day of my burial.* ⁸*You will always have the poor among you, but you will not always have me."*

My church is not architecturally special, but it does have a wonderful woodwork. The roof is splendid: it is not the roof of a cathedral but the wooden roof of craftsmen. It is functional yet beautiful, with many intersecting wooden beams. Many visitors have commented that it looks like an inverted boat. There are also beautiful wooden carvings on the pulpit, altar rail and reredos. Many churches have items of great beauty in them. It may be the stained glass windows, or the use of stone, or a wonderful painting. At some time people sat down and planned their church and did all they could to make it beautiful. It was no different with the tabernacle in Exodus 31.

This reading is one that is often used to justify artistic work in church and also a reading to inspire it. Bezalel, Oholiab and the craftsmen were called to make the tabernacle, everything in it and the garments for the priests. It was a work of building, carpentry, metalwork, weaving and tailoring. It was a very wide artistic enterprise. It is evidence that God cares about aesthetics and beauty. So how did they go about it?

First of all there is the selection of the men for the work. The work in the tabernacle is so important it needs a special appointment of a man filled with the Holy Spirit: Bezalel. He is chosen by God and Oholiab is chosen as his deputy. Sometimes Bezalel has been thought of as an architect but he is not. The architect is God; the blueprint with all the necessary details for the tabernacle is laid down by God. Rather Bezalel is a skilled builder who interprets the architects plan. There is actually little room for creativity here. Rather he is a craftsman.

Secondly Bezalel is filled with the Holy Spirit. The task God has chosen for him requires God's own power and strength. Bezalel is one of the very few people in the Old Testament filled with God. It is a sign of the importance of the task.

What does God give him? Precisely what he needs for the task: "skill, ability and knowledge" (v.3). Perhaps this can be interpreted slightly differently:
- wisdom (the gift to understand what is needed to fulfil God's instructions)
- discernment (the talent for solving the problems that were bound to come up)
- skill (which was needed to guide and accomplish the work itself)

In short, when it is God calling us to a task, he will give us what we need for the job.

Thirdly God gave him an assistant, Oholiab. It is very easy to think we can work alone or lead alone. Usually an assistant is needed for the work to succeed. Both the leader and the deputy need to know their place and respect one another if the project is to succeed. It is notable that Oholiab is also divinely appointed.

Finally there are the craftsmen to whom God has also given skill. What exactly does this mean? Were they unskilled but became skilled by God's gifting? It seems unlikely because that is not the plain sense of the verse. It is not said they were given a special, new gifting (like Bezalel). Rather I think they were craftsmen whose original skill was God-given. Here we have an example of there being "natural" gifts from birth honed by training that are equally gifts from God for his work. This is a very early text of the activity of God among his people giving gifts and a sign that not all gifts are specially given by a "miraculous" work of the Holy Spirit.

This speaks directly to those exercising "charismatic" gifts today in God's Church. All of our talents are God-given and all of them are intended for his glory. There are times when we are called to use all the faculties we have for him. Nevertheless there are also times when he will specially enable someone for a task where they didn't have the skills previously; such was Bezalel.

The temple of Solomon that succeeded the tabernacle was more ornate, more expensive and more impressive that the tabernacle. It was meant to be. Solomon chose the best of everything, because he recognised that his God was greater than all others (2 Chronicles 2:5). We can read about the materials he used and the cost of the whole project in the first chapters of 2 Chronicles. And it seemed that God was pleased with this for he says he has chosen and consecrated the temple (2 Chronicles 7:16). Many today would be appalled at such a "wastage". There is a lack of understanding in the modern utilitarian western world that doing something that honours God is not wasted. The cathedrals of medieval England are seen as wonderful but impractical, not to be repeated.

Yet even in today's society there are times when things are just done for show. The opening of an Olympic Games is notoriously expensive but all host countries expect their country to be shown at its best. In the whole area of sport vast sums are spent on stadia that could be used for health or the poor but there is little complaint. Stadia are made massive and beautiful by their architects and owners. Another example of national pride and expense was the space race. Although material benefits did accrue, they were not certain at the time. Rather the pride of seeing a magnificent rocket go into space and astronauts achieve a difficult mission was sufficient. In modern society it is not that prestigious and expensive projects lack support; rather people cannot see the point of doing it for God.

A key text for Christians in trying to decide how much they

pay towards artistic endeavour and how much towards the practical help of people is John 12. Here Mary "wastes" a huge amount of money on a gesture. The amount is equivalent to one years' wages. It is an astonishing gift, contrasted with Judas' attitude of false care for the poor masking his theft.

From Jesus response we see that feeding the poor is not the highest activity for a Christian. The highest is glorifying Jesus in whatever way we can. Often that will be through practical giving and help. But equally there will be times when it will be in creating an artistic monument to him: a stained glass window or a piece of art.

How can we tell where God is leading us? Is it to give to the poor or making something beautiful? The defining factor is motivation. Why are we doing it? But a second factor is gifting and availability. As with Bezalel, Oholiab and the craftsmen, if God's wants a building for his worship, he will give the guidance and resources necessary. He will also direct us to show us how best to glorify him.

**Questions to consider**

How much is a years' wages to you? Would you consider giving so much?

How is your church decorated? Does it honour God?

How legitimate is it to spend time and money on buildings?

If the temple today is made up of the people of God (where God resides) shouldn't we spend more time on people?

# 10. The Day of Atonement

*Leviticus 16:1-2, 11-34*

<sup>1</sup>*The LORD spoke to Moses after the death of the two sons of Aaron who died when they approached the LORD.* <sup>2</sup>*The LORD said to Moses: "Tell your brother Aaron not to come whenever he chooses into the Most Holy Place behind the curtain in front of the atonement cover on the ark, or else he will die, because I appear in the cloud over the atonement cover.*

<sup>11</sup>*"Aaron shall bring the bull for his own sin offering to make atonement for himself and his household, and he is to slaughter the bull for his own sin offering.* <sup>12</sup>*He is to take a censer full of burning coals from the altar before the LORD and two handfuls of finely ground fragrant incense and take them behind the curtain.* <sup>13</sup>*He is to put the incense on the fire before the LORD, and the smoke of the incense will conceal the atonement cover above the Testimony, so that he will not die.* <sup>14</sup>*He is to take some of the bull's blood and with his finger sprinkle it on the front of the atonement cover; then he shall sprinkle some of it with his finger seven times before the atonement cover.*

<sup>15</sup>*"He shall then slaughter the goat for the sin offering for the people and take its blood behind the curtain and do with it as he did with the bull's blood: He shall sprinkle it on the atonement cover and in front of it.* <sup>16</sup>*In this way he will make atonement for the Most Holy Place because of the uncleanness and rebellion of the Israelites, whatever their sins have been. He is to do the same for the Tent of Meeting, which is among them in the midst of their uncleanness.* <sup>17</sup>*No-one is to be in the Tent of Meeting from the time Aaron goes in to make atonement in the Most Holy Place until he comes out, having made atonement for himself, his household and the whole community of Israel.*

<sup>18</sup>*"Then he shall come out to the altar that is before the LORD*

and make atonement for it. He shall take some of the bull's blood and some of the goat's blood and put it on all the horns of the altar. [19]He shall sprinkle some of the blood on it with his finger seven times to cleanse it and consecrate it from the uncleanness of the Israelites.

[20]"When Aaron has finished making atonement for the Most Holy Place, the Tent of Meeting and the altar, he shall bring forward the live goat. [21]He is to lay both hands on the head of the live goat and confess over it all the wickedness and rebellion of the Israelites—all their sins—and put them on the goat's head. He shall send the goat away into the desert in the care of a man appointed for the task. [22]The goat will carry on itself all their sins to a solitary place; and the man shall release it in the desert.

[23]"Then Aaron is to go into the Tent of Meeting and take off the linen garments he put on before he entered the Most Holy Place, and he is to leave them there. [24]He shall bathe himself with water in a holy place and put on his regular garments. Then he shall come out and sacrifice the burnt offering for himself and the burnt offering for the people, to make atonement for himself and for the people. [25]He shall also burn the fat of the sin offering on the altar.

[26]"The man who releases the goat as a scapegoat must wash his clothes and bathe himself with water; afterwards he may come into the camp. [27]The bull and the goat for the sin offerings, whose blood was brought into the Most Holy Place to make atonement, must be taken outside the camp; their hides, flesh and offal are to be burned up. [28]The man who burns them must wash his clothes and bathe himself with water; afterwards he may come into the camp.

[29]"This is to be a lasting ordinance for you: On the tenth day of the seventh month you must deny yourselves and not do any work—whether native-born or an alien living among you— [30]because on this day atonement will be made for you, to cleanse you. Then, before the LORD, you will be clean from all your sins. [31]It is a sabbath of rest, and you must deny yourselves; it is a lasting ordinance. [32]The priest

> *who is anointed and ordained to succeed his father as high*
> *priest is to make atonement. He is to put on the sacred linen*
> *garments* [33] *and make atonement for the Most Holy Place, for*
> *the Tent of Meeting and the altar, and for the priests and all*
> *the people of the community.*
> [34] *"This is to be a lasting ordinance for you: Atonement is to*
> *be made once a year for all the sins of the Israelites."*
> *And it was done, as the* LORD *commanded Moses.*

Leviticus 16 is the most important biblical text concerning the most important subject for the tabernacle: atonement. Leviticus 16 happens to be in the very centre of Leviticus and in the very centre of the Pentateuch. It is an appropriate place, for it is central in all Jewish practice in the Old Testament and central for our understanding of Jesus.

Two of Aaron's four sons, Nadab and Abihu, offered unauthorised incense before the Lord in the Holy of Holies. They were immediately consumed by the fire of the Lord and died. (The story can be found in Leviticus 10.) This is the background to the command to Aaron in verses 1 and 2 of chapter 16. Those who approach God must be holy and honour him. A general outline of how to do this is given in verses 3-10; the rest of chapter 16 gives more detail to the rituals.

So what was the spiritual purpose of the Day of Atonement? There were three aspects.

1. The sin and whole offerings expiated the sins of the priests and the entire congregation. In the text we see that Aaron offered a bull in sacrifice to atone for his own sins and the sins of his household (v.11). With the blood of the bull and the censer of incense he could enter the Holy of Holies (the Most Holy Place) behind the curtain and sprinkle blood on the "atonement cover" (v.15). The atonement cover is also known as "the mercy seat". It is the cover over the Ark of the Covenant below the two cherubim. It was seen as the very throne of Yahweh where he reigned in the Holy of Holies.

The mercy seat covered the stone tablets of the law that rested in the Ark of the Covenant and was itself shadowed by the wings of the angels, the messengers of God. Therefore the blood sacrifice directly restored the covenant relationship between God and his people after their sin.

A second sin sacrifice was that of a goat for all the people. The goat was sacrificed on the main altar in the courtyard and then the High Priest re-entered the Holy of Holies to sprinkle the blood of the goat as he had done with the bull (v.16). Later the High Priest also offered up burnt offerings for the priests and people (v.24) to make atonement, although precisely for what is not said.

The whole idea of blood sacrifice is difficult for us to accept today and it stands in the way of some accepting the Christian faith. People tend to find blood sacrifice wasteful (which is actually true of any sacrifice). There is also a great difficulty in seeing any real spiritual connection. It is far too physical for western spirituality. Furthermore blood sacrifice is seen as morally and spiritually revolting, a sign of past monstrosities we no longer accept. These objections are very deep-seated yet the subject is essential to our Christian belief. As we know, Jesus was the ultimate blood sacrifice. So how can we address them?

First of all we need to realise that much in these objections is culturally bound. Most cultures, in most parts of the world throughout history, instinctively understood this process of blood sacrifice. Yet we do not. Take for example the issue of sacrifice being wasteful. It is not if it pleases God; it is the secular dismissal of God that immediately makes the process wasteful.

What about the problem of seeing anything spiritual in blood sacrifice? The modern concept of spirituality is very ephemeral. Often it is seen to be about feelings, individuality, and mystery. However, true spirituality is about connecting with God. This includes obedience, discipleship and fellowship. The sacrifice was a gift to God in obedience. It was also done in community and acted as purification for the community. Within that there was a great mystery (behind the veil), a feeling of celebration and a sense of individual forgiveness. Any true spirituality needs to include the communal as well as the individual, the practical as well as the mysterious.

61

Modern antipathy to killing animals is very widespread: an urban concern of the West (which is far removed from the process of butchery) and also a religious concern of Hindus and Buddhists, among others. Nevertheless most cultures killed animals in the past. This even included Hindus in medieval times for blood sacrifice. It is possible vegetarians to tolerate the killing of animals if, for example, someone is in danger from the animal. Of course in the sacrificial process the emphasis is never on the eating of meat but in pleasing God. Yet this brings in perhaps the greatest obstacle of all. The animal is innocent. It hasn't done anything deserving of death. How can God be demanding what appears to be an immoral act?

There are a number of answers to this complaint. The first is that God commanded it, he is good and he knows best. This may all be true but it is hardly satisfying to a modern sceptic! The second is that we are commanded to be good stewards of nature. We are called to organise and care for the natural world rather than assume that all in the natural world is simply "good". (Within this animals have a significant purpose but it is important not to over sentimentalise them. We have a moral duty (under God) not to ill treat them and animals can (and do) show us God's creativity and wonder.) The third (and most telling to me) is that within the culture of Moses and the Israelites these objections would have seemed astonishing, even non-sensical. God was working with them where they were and at the same time pointing forward to the one great sacrifice of his own. Christians do not (and never have) indulged in blood sacrifice. In his developing revelation God has showed his true purpose for sacrifice: that he would be his own sacrifice. He would expiate the sins of the people permanently, once and for all.

2. The second purpose for sacrifice was to cleanse the whole sanctuary from the pollution caused by the sins of the people. The tabernacle was used for sacrifice throughout the year; the Day of Atonement was the day it was cleansed. "He (the High Priest) will make atonement for the Most Holy Place because of the uncleanness and rebellion of the Israelites" (v.16). When Aaron daubed the horns of the altar with blood it was to clean it (v.18). Although it may seem difficult to us that something can be made clean when

blood is smeared on it, in fact there is a modern concept that helps us: that of pollution. The blood is acting as an anti-pollutant. The pollution in this case is obviously spiritual, not biological. Through sacrifice cleansing is obtained.

3. The third spiritual purpose of the day was to remove the sins of the people and liability for them entirely from the community. In v.21 we read that a second goat is brought to the High Priest who lays hands on it and confesses the sins of the people and priests—their wickedness, rebellion and sin. In other words all kinds of sin were included. The goat was then released and sent into the desert. It carried the sin of the community and thus broke their capacity for causing harm or disharmony. The goat was known as the "scapegoat" (v.8, 26). This goat could not be sacrificed as it was unclean, but rather it died in the desert. In concept modern readers can understand this well. There is a psychological need to place our forgiven wrong-doing on something else in order to know it has really gone. At its worst this is what happens when someone displaces their own wrong doing by blaming exactly the same thing on someone else. Rather better is the use of penance after confession, which can channel our forgiven sins into something practical. But best of all is the spiritual practice of prayerfully giving everything to Christ as we come to him for forgiveness. He acts as a scapegoat as well as a blood sacrifice.

**Questions to consider**

Read Hebrews 9:1 to 10:14. List the way Jesus fulfils the Day of Atonement.

# 11. The Temple Layout

*Exodus 26:30-27:1*

[30]*"Set up the tabernacle according to the plan shown you on the mountain.* [31]*"Make a curtain of blue, purple and scarlet yarn and finely twisted linen, with cherubim worked into it by a skilled craftsman.* [32]*Hang it with gold hooks on four posts of acacia wood overlaid with gold and standing on four silver bases.* [33]*Hang the curtain from the clasps and place the ark of the Testimony behind the curtain. The curtain will separate the Holy Place from the Most Holy Place.* [34]*Put the atonement cover on the ark of the Testimony in the Most Holy Place.* [35]*Place the table outside the curtain on the north side of the tabernacle and put the lampstand opposite it on the south side.* [36]*"For the entrance to the tent make a curtain of blue, purple and scarlet yarn and finely twisted linen—the work of an embroiderer.* [37]*Make gold hooks for this curtain and five posts of acacia wood overlaid with gold. And cast five bronze bases for them.* [1]*"Build an altar of acacia wood, three cubits high; it is to be square, five cubits long and five cubits wide".*

*from 2 Chronicles 3 and 4:1*

[1]*Then Solomon began to build the temple of the L*ORD *in Jerusalem on Mount Moriah...*[4]*he overlaid the inside with pure gold...* [7]*and he carved cherubim on the walls...*[8]*He built the Most Holy Place...*[10]*in (it) he made a pair of sculptured cherubim...*[14]*he made the curtain of blue, purple and crimson yarn and fine linen, with cherubim worked into it...*[1]*He made a bronze altar.*

*Luke 1:9-10*

[9]*(Zechariah) was chosen by lot, according to the custom of the priesthood, to go into the temple of the Lord and burn incense.* [10]*And when the time for the burning of incense came, all the assembled worshippers were praying outside.*

My wife is Jordanian. Her parent's old house in Amman followed a pattern typical of many Arab homes in the past and present. When you entered the door the first room to greet you was a reception room. Here was the best furniture, different packets of cigarettes for the choice of the visitor, sugared nuts and wrapped chocolates. The family almost never use this room. Going further in the next room was the living/dining room, the place for the family to gather. Finally, beyond that and out of sight, are the bedrooms and bathroom. The whole layout of the house is structured around visitors and is made up of three parts. The further in you go, the closer you come to the heart of the family life, even though the place of greatest honour is on the outside. Architecture reflects the relationships in the society and gives meaning to the living space.

The tabernacle and succeeding temples were similar in that they had a basic tripartite structure. The later temples all deliberately copied the original tabernacle. The tent that made up the tabernacle was divided into two by a great curtain. On one side, next to the entrance, was the Holy Place. On the far side, furthest in, was the Most Holy Place (or Holy of Holies). The entrance itself also had a great curtain in front of it. The tabernacle stood in a courtyard, and in the courtyard, near to the entrance of the tabernacle, stood the altar. Thus there were three stages in the structure of the tabernacle, going from the outside in: the courtyard with the altar; the Holy Place; and the Most Holy Place.

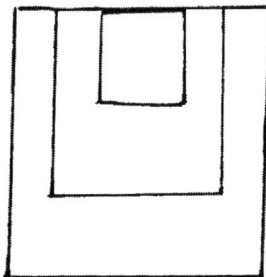

Solomon's temple was very similar, although it was made of stone. On the outside was the courtyard, where the altar stood. As one entered, you went into the Holy Place, and then behind the curtain was the Most Holy Place. There was also a similar positioning of the contents. The ark of the Testimony stood inside the Most Holy Place, with two statues of cherubim either side, their wings overshadowing the ark. In the Holy Place stood the lampstand.

The so-called second temple, the one made by Herod the Great, had a similar structure, although it was greatly elaborated upon. The court of the temple still had the Most Holy Place, the Holy Place, and the courtyard with the altar, all separated by great curtains. Zechariah (Luke 1:9-10) burned incense on the altar before the sacrifice of the animals at the same place. Now, however, there are additional courts beyond, for different categories of people. Even here there is tripartite structure, for beyond the court already described was the women's court and the court of the gentiles.

Why is there this elaborate structure? No less than in my in-law's home, it reflects an essential reality. The outer court represented the place where humanity dwelt; the Holy Place symbolised the visible heavens; the Most Holy Place the invisible part of the heavens, where God and his angels lived. There was thus an increase of holiness from the outer court towards the Most Holy Place. There was also a change in the people allowed in each area: all the people of Israel in the outer court (although this was divided up in Herod's temple, as we have seen); priests in the Holy Place; and the High Priest in the Most Holy Place.

This idea is reinforced by the furnishings in the temple. The bronze sea and the altar for burnt offerings are in the outer court. The bronze sea was a direct reminder of the sea itself, whilst the altar was rooted in the earth and sacrifice of animals. The decorations in the outer court (such as bulls supporting the wash basins) also support this idea. In the Holy Place were the lampstands, the "lights", which is the word used for the sun and moon in Genesis. In Revelation 1:20 the seven lamps on the lampstand are represented by an angel, who is shown as a star. The two curtains separating the areas are woven in two shades of blue and red. We learn from Josephus, speaking of Herod's temple, that the blue and purple represented the blue of the sky and the dark blue of the clouds. Perhaps the red was meant to be the setting sun. It is notable that the same colours are used for each temple. Even the priest's robes reflect this idea. Their robes were dark blue, with use of the same colours in the curtains, with precious stone in the breastplate (Exodus 28:15-33). In the Most Holy Place the two cherubim are above the ark, and figures of angels are woven into the curtain that guards the sanctuary. Furthermore, no human could enter into the presence of the glory of God. The High Priest himself, who entered once a year, only did so by offering a cloud of incense so thick that he could not see God's appearance (Leviticus 16:13). The Ark of the Covenant itself was understood to be the footstool of God's heavenly throne (Psalm 99:5, Psalm 132:7-8).

What is the importance for us today in this structure of the temple? There are a number of lessons we need to learn. One is the difference between the Israelite temple and those of the surrounding peoples. They too often had a similar structure, but in their Most Holy Place there was an idol, and in the Holy Place the astrological signs were much more prominent. Magic and idol worship were central. In Yahweh's temple, he could never be seen. He was too great, too awesome. This was a wonder to all of the pagan peoples who knew the Jews, down to Roman times. We need to rediscover the greatness of God, and not be sucked into the idol worship and superstition that is developing all around us.

We live in a culture of familiarity and friendship, of individual rights and access to authority (at least, in theory!). If we wish to see our M.P., we can. If we wish to visit Buckingham Palace, we can. Furthermore, money talks. With enough money we can gain access and power to virtually anywhere. The Most Holy Place teaches us of a great God. If we look on him, we will die. If we approach him without reverence, we are sinning greatly. We sing, "What a friend we have in Jesus", and it is true. We also sing of the greatness of God, for he is far above us. In Protestant belief there is access to God and we can approach him. This so often leads us into complacency; we begin to take it for granted. Perhaps the pendulum has swung too far.

The sad truth is we often no longer value sufficiently the work Jesus did for us in opening up the Most Holy Place and allowing us into God's presence. We simply saunter in, as if we are entering our bedroom. Here is the great difference between my in-law's house and the temple: their inner sanctuary was simply private, not glorious. When we stayed as a family I can say without fear of contradiction that the bedroom was extremely inglorious!

It was the Protestant revolution that began the move towards equality, freedom and individualism. Our church buildings reflect that. We see in most Anglican churches that the rood screen has been dismantled, and there is only a simple communion rail. In Reformed and Baptist churches there is not even that. However it is different in the Orthodox Church. Here a typical building is styled along the lines of the temple. The body of the church is for all the worshippers; above the apse, where the bread is distributed, is a blue sky with stars. But further in there is the iconostasis, which divides the priests from the people. Here the celebration of the Eucharist takes place, hidden, in mystery and awe.

It is not necessary to return to Orthodox worship to recognise that in much of our public worship in western churches we have lost a sense of awe and wonder. It would be valuable to relearn in public worship the mystery of God and to appreciate how much it cost Jesus to give us that access to God. It certainly is essential in our relationship with God day by day.

### Questions to consider
How do you approach God?
Where can we see the greatness of God today?
How does our culture ignore his majesty?
Do you have idols that replace him?

# 12. The Word from the Temple

*Isaiah 6:1-10*

*¹In the year that King Uzziah died, I saw the Lord seated on a throne, high and exalted, and the train of his robe filled the temple. ²Above him were seraphs, each with six wings: With two wings they covered their faces, with two they covered their feet, and with two they were flying. ³And they were calling to one another: "Holy, holy, holy is the LORD Almighty; the whole earth is full of his glory." ⁴At the sound of their voices the door-posts and thresholds shook and the temple was filled with smoke. ⁵"Woe to me!" I cried. "I am ruined! For I am a man of unclean lips, and I live among a people of unclean lips, and my eyes have seen the King, the LORD Almighty." ⁶Then one of the seraphs flew to me with a live coal in his hand, which he had taken with tongs from the altar. ⁷With it he touched my mouth and said, "See, this has touched your lips; your guilt is taken away and your sin atoned for." ⁸Then I heard the voice of the Lord saying, "Whom shall I send? And who will go for us?" And I said, "Here am I. Send me!" ⁹He said, "Go and tell this people: "'Be ever hearing, but never understanding; be ever seeing, but never perceiving.' ¹⁰ Make the heart of this people calloused; make their ears dull and close their eyes. Otherwise they might see with their eyes, hear with their ears, understand with their hearts, and turn and be healed."*

*Luke 10:1-12*

*¹After this the Lord appointed seventy–two others and sent them two by two ahead of him to every town and place where he was about to go. ²He told them, "The harvest is plentiful, but the workers are few. Ask the Lord of the harvest, therefore, to send out workers into his harvest field. ³Go! I am sending you out like lambs among wolves. ⁴Do not take a purse or bag or sandals; and do not greet anyone on the road. ⁵"When you enter a house, first say, 'Peace to this house.' ⁶If a man of peace is there, your peace will rest on him; if not, it will return to you. ⁷Stay in that house, eating and drinking whatever they give you, for the worker deserves his wages. Do not move around from house to house. ⁸"When you enter a town and are welcomed, eat what is set before you. ⁹Heal the sick who are there and tell them, 'The kingdom of God is near you.' ¹⁰But when you enter a town and are not welcomed, go into its streets and say, ¹¹'Even the dust of your town that sticks to our feet we wipe off against you. Yet be sure of this: The kingdom of God is near.' ¹²I tell you, it will be more bearable on that day for Sodom than for that town.*

There is a scene in the Sound of Music where Maria (the nun played by Julie Andrews) is about to leave the convent to get married. She is surrounded by the other nuns but instead of being dressed in black she is now dressed in pure white. Her wedding robe has a great train that seems to fill the enclosed space behind the metal gates. Then the Mother Superior takes out her keys, unlocks the gates, and Maria glides forth into the great cathedral to meet her husband. From there she goes forth into the world to meet danger and challenge but no longer in the enclosed world of the convent.

It is rather fanciful to compare the Sound of Music with the great commissioning of Isaiah in Isaiah 6, but there are a number of similarities, and not just the idea of a large train of a gown. The main similarity is the idea of going forth from an enclosed space into the whole world. Anyone in a monastic order will tell you that they are not divorced from the "real" world; rather they probably see it more clearly than those of us in the world. Through prayer and contemplation they can perceive God's view of his world. Nevertheless they are not in the world and the world has to come to them to receive their wisdom.

The temple of the Lord was rather similar. God had deliberately put himself in a place where he guaranteed to be, namely the temple in Jerusalem, and before that in the tabernacle. Isaiah saw him in a vision, seated on his throne (presumably on or above the Ark of the Covenant) and his glory was so great that the train of his robe filled the temple. This is an image that, though overwhelming, was consistent with the established concept of God in his temple. However we then have a number of remarkable incidents that show God going forth from his temple in his glory. A little like Maria, the gates are unlocked and God goes forth. God dispenses with his self-imposed seclusion and his mission goes into the whole world.

This is, of course, to simplify greatly, and the first indication that this is too simplistic a notion comes in the song of the seraphim, "Holy, holy, holy is the Lord Almighty; the whole earth is full of his glory." Already the earth is full of his glory, and although the text does tell us how his glory is throughout the world we can see it in other parts of the Bible. The whole of creation shows the glory of the creator God. His intervention into history speaks of his sovereignty. The giving of the law to Moses reveals his will for humankind. The specific incidents, prior to Isaiah, where he has spoken to humans (Elijah for example) showed his majesty. God was always in his world.

Nevertheless something different is happening here. This incident is not only about Isaiah being commissioned. Here we have a prefiguring of the whole movement of God by his incarnation in Bethlehem and the sending of his Holy Spirit at Pentecost. We have a precursor of the mission of Christ. First of all we read that the whole temple is shaken and filled with smoke. The shaking is not destruction but it is a sign that the temple cannot possibly contain God. He is beyond a simple building. When all is said and done, Solomon's temple was only a building. It was a fine building, built to the very highest standard with the very best materials, according to the commands of God himself; but it was only a building. Other temples to other gods were built all over the area in different places and at different times. Many of these were equally splendid, at least to human eyes. When God came into his world in his full glory, as his incarnated son Jesus, he left the confines of the temple and of heaven. He issued forth into his world with his mission for all humanity. He also predicted the destruction of his temple and the building of a new one, not with human hands. All this is the subject of other chapters. Here in Isaiah we see the shaking of the temple, the sign that the temple on earth is not eternal but merely a stage in the far greater story of the mission of God.

The second "going forth" is through a seraph taking a "live" coal from the altar and touching Isaiah's lips with it. In this whole episode fire plays a very important part. The word "seraph" literally means "burning one". The smoke surrounding the holy God suggests fire. The word "holy" itself indicates brightness. In general this speaks of the separateness of God and the creatures in his attendance; in particular it indicates judgement. The fire of the altar is not a cleansing or purifying agent but rather represents the wrath of God because of his unapproachable holiness. Typical of what fire means is found in Numbers 11:1, "Then the fire from the Lord burned among them and consumed some of the outskirts of the camp". The coal is taken from the altar where the blood sacrifice was made, a sacrifice which God consumed as an offering for sin. The coal thus becomes the agent of both judgement and redemption at the same time; at the altar outside the temple judgement comes upon the sin offering rather than the people. In this simple "live" coal we have the great themes of atonement and propitiation for sin which are required by a holy God and at the same time the forgiveness and reconciliation that are needed by his people. The coal is thus the agent of the holy and pure God which accepts the blood sacrifice.

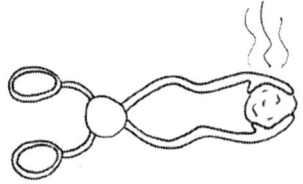

The seraph takes the coal in tongs and touches Isaiah's mouth with it. This is in response to Isaiah's cry of inadequacy and sinfulness. He knows his ruination; no-one can see God and live. He knows that his own voice is impure. He has heard the worship songs of the seraphim and knows that his worship, however good in human eyes, is nothing short of sinful. He also recognises that in all this he is representative of all his people: "I am a man of unclean lips and I live among a people of unclean lips". From his perspective there is no hope once he has seen the majesty of God. He is simply ruined. One of the tragedies of our modern western life is the loss of awe when considering God. Christians are not exempt as we are all affected by our culture. We too are a people of unclean lips, but often we do not recognise it.

When the coal touches Isaiah's lips it has an amazing effect. "Your guilt is taken away and your sin atoned for". This is not a mere symbol; the coal is the active agent of real forgiveness. God in his grace meets Isaiah. All Isaiah does is cry out concerning his sin. The response from God is a free gift. Isaiah does nothing to deserve it, let alone give anything in return. This is the grace of God. God meets him at the point of his confessed need, the sinfulness of his lips, yet there is forgiveness for his whole person. The effect of the coal is instantaneous; there is removal of guilt and atonement immediately. Yet all this comes about through the payment of a price. "Atonement" can only occur when a ransom price is paid and justice accomplished; that is the meaning of the word. Where is the payment on this occasion? Since the coal came from the altar of sacrifice we know that there was a sacrifice as prescribed by the law. But what was the sacrifice? It could simply be the normal sacrifice in the temple but the stature of the vision and the presence of God "high and exalted" show that this is one of the occasions where heaven intersects with earth. In the heavenly realm there is only one permanent sacrifice, and that is the sacrifice of Christ on the cross. Isaiah sees no hint of this at that time, but with the perspective of all God's work we can see a prefiguring of the mission of Jesus and his sacrificial work on the cross.

However in his later prophecies Isaiah begins to see what this sacrifice was. Of all the Old Testament Prophets the book of Isaiah has the greatest revelation of the work of the Messiah as a suffering servant. As the prophetic ministry unfolded God gave messages like Isaiah 53, "He was despised and rejected by men, a man of sorrows…he was pierced for our transgressions, he was crushed for our iniquities; the punishment that brought us peace was upon him…the Lord has laid on him the iniquity of us all." The way in which the atonement Isaiah received is carried out begins to be seen in the book that carries his name. It will be through a suffering servant who will carry the sin of all and so bring peace with God.

The third "going forth" by God is through his newly commissioned prophet, Isaiah. Following his reconciliation with God Isaiah hears his voice for the first time: "Whom shall I send, and who shall go for us?" Who is the "us" in this question? The New Testament quotes this passage twice to give us the answer. John 12:41 says, "Isaiah said this because he saw Jesus' glory and spoke about him". Acts 28:25 says, "The Holy Spirit spoke the truth to your forefathers when he said through Isaiah the prophet: 'Go to this people and say…'". In other words the "us" is taken by the New Testament writers to include both the Holy Spirit and Jesus. This is one of the clearest statements about the Holy Trinity in the scriptures. At one and the same time God can say, referring to himself, "I" and "us". The holiness of God exists in a community of love that still has a single unity.

Isaiah, with purified lips, now has the ability to speak before Almighty God: "Here am I; send me!" Isaiah now volunteers where he would never have been brave enough (nor adequate enough) before. He is prepared in his heart to give complete service to God following his wonderful atonement. This flow of grace and response is the precise opposite of duty-bound Christianity that once was so common. Duty is a fine thing but unless it comes from an origin of an experience of the grace of God it will soon be transformed into a sullen obedience that can never glorify God. Indeed there needs to be many experiences of God's grace to feed the sacrifice to which dutiful Christians are called. The calling of Isaiah is to prophecy. "Go tell this people…" he is commanded. In this way, through the prophecy of Isaiah, the word goes forth from the temple. Once again it is a precursor of when the Word came forth from the Godhead in the person of Jesus the Messiah. Isaiah bears the word of God to his people; Jesus was the Word itself. He is the embodiment of the Word of God.

Jesus himself sent his disciples out bearing his word. The story of the seventy-two in Luke 10 is only one example. It is clear from these two passages that bearing God's word is no easy thing. Isaiah is told that he is going to speak to make the ears of the people unhearing, the eyes unseeing and their hearts without understanding so that they do not repent! This is a very strange objective for a communicator! Yet a glance through the book of Isaiah shows that Isaiah's words were plain and simple to understand. It is not that God was deliberately giving a difficult message so that the people could not respond and therefore be condemned. Rather the people were given every opportunity to respond by God but nevertheless they rejected him. Chapters 7-11 of Isaiah show just how the message was rejected. Nevertheless within the rejection God still gives his people a message of hope for the remnant that remain, particularly concerning his Messiah to come (Isaiah 9:1-7 and Isaiah 11).

The disciples had a similar mixed task and response. However the situation was now different. Jesus tells them that the harvest is plentiful but the workers few. They are sent out to reap the harvest but in the knowledge that they will face opposition. They are to be bearers of the grace of God in word and deed and so bring the Kingdom of God to people's towns and homes; yet when they are rejected there is the inevitability of judgement for that place. We see in the ministry of Jesus and his disciples a great response. There is the feeding of the 5000 and the acclamation of the crowds when he entered Jerusalem. One could say that this was very "successful", except that almost everyone melted away when he was crucified. After the resurrection, the eyes of many were reopened and the Jesus movement grew in number. Nevertheless it is significant where the growth came from. Initially many were Jews but then Jewish opposition grew. Larger numbers came from the marginalised Samaria (where Jesus and the disciples had seen a remarkable response in John 4) and then from the Gentiles, having the opportunity to be full members of the Kingdom of God for the first time. Rather like the time of Isaiah many of the people Jesus came to ended up with blinded eyes and unhearing ears. In fact he even used Isaiah 6:9-10 to describe what would happen when he taught in parables (Mark 4:12).

It is similar today when the word proceeds from God into his world. The carriers of the word need to recognise their inadequacy and know the grace of the forgiveness of God. Even so our task is to respond to God's command, not to see what we would call "success". The harvest fields may be plentiful or the hearts of the hearers may be hardened (to mix biblical metaphors!). We may see substantial response or we may see people turning away or even persecuting the messenger (as happened to many prophets, the disciples and Jesus himself). We are responsible for our own failings, our foolishness in tactics or our clumsiness in presentation. Nevertheless even perfect communication through perfect obedience and the power of the Holy Spirit does not ensure people respond to the word God sends. That is what Isaiah experienced. Too often there is a triumphalist tone to mission, an assumption that obedience and faithfulness to God's command is bound to lead to what we call "success". The opposite may be true and should not be a barrier to the obedience to the command to go out into all the world. God has ensured that his word will proceed from his Holy Place and, one way or another, there will be a culmination of grace and judgement. Our task is to humbly obey and trust God.

To return to the Sound of Music, Maria went out from the Cathedral to a mission of marriage, motherhood, danger and singing. "Climb every mountain" may not be the most Christian song but it does have a sense of the Christian vocation in the first line: God's calling for us is to follow him over mountain and through stream for the sake of the message of his kingdom.

## Questions to consider

Put yourself in Isaiah's place (perhaps by reading the passage very slowly). How do you feel?

Why can speaking God's word be so difficult?

How does God want you to go out with his word?

# 13. The Destruction of the Temple

*Jeremiah 7:3-15*

<sup>3</sup>"*This is what the* LORD *Almighty, the God of Israel, says: 'Reform your ways and your actions, and I will let you live in this place.* <sup>4</sup>*Do not trust in deceptive words and say, "This is the temple of the* LORD, *the temple of the* LORD, *the temple of the* LORD!*"* <sup>5</sup>*If you really change your ways and your actions and deal with each other justly,* <sup>6</sup>*if you do not oppress the alien, the fatherless or the widow and do not shed innocent blood in this place, and if you do not follow other gods to your own harm,* <sup>7</sup>*then I will let you live in this place, in the land I gave your forefathers for ever and ever.* <sup>8</sup>*But look, you are trusting in deceptive words that are worthless.* <sup>9</sup>*"'Will you steal and murder, commit adultery and perjury, burn incense to Baal and follow other gods you have not known,* <sup>10</sup>*and then come and stand before me in this house, which bears my Name, and say, "We are safe"—safe to do all these detestable things?* <sup>11</sup>*Has this house, which bears my Name, become a den of robbers to you? But I have been watching! declares the* LORD. <sup>12</sup>*"'Go now to the place in Shiloh where I first made a dwelling for my Name, and see what I did to it because of the wickedness of my people Israel.* <sup>13</sup>*While you were doing all these things, declares the* LORD, *I spoke to you again and again, but you did not listen; I called you, but you did not answer.* <sup>14</sup>*Therefore, what I did to Shiloh I will now do to the house that bears my Name, the temple you trust in, the place I gave to you and your fathers.* <sup>15</sup>*I will thrust you from my presence, just as I did all your brothers, the people of Ephraim.'"*

*Matthew 21:12-13*

<sup>12</sup>*Jesus entered the temple area and drove out all who were buying and selling there. He overturned the tables of the money-changers and the benches of those selling doves.* <sup>13</sup>*"It*

> *is written,"* he said to them, " *'My house will be called a house of prayer,' but you are making it a* **'den of robbers'.** "

*Matthew 26:61*

> [61] *"This fellow said, 'I am able to destroy the temple of God and rebuild it in three days.' "*

*Psalm 137:1*

> [1] *By the rivers of Babylon we sat and wept when we remembered Zion.*

The headline in my local paper said this, *"Ten churches face closure"*. There were pictures of each one of them on the inside pages, but the largest was for the most prominent, St. Peter's. A Mr. Peter Beal, great great grandson of a couple who have a memorial plaque in the church was quoted as saying, "I am not religious but I am sad this is happening, it's a wonderful old church and an important part of history. Something should be done to stop this".

It is always sad when churches close, and especially if we can look back to a time when the glory of God was apparent. And it may well be that the closure of churches is a judgement on our failure to proclaim the gospel to our generation. However the closure of a church, no matter how wonderful that church was, is nothing to the destruction of the temple. And any judgement of God that we may feel is nothing to the judgement that fell on the people when the temple was destroyed.

The temple was destroyed and rebuilt more than once. The reading from Jeremiah tells us of the destruction of the temple at Shiloh. The prophecy in Jeremiah of the destruction of Solomon's temple in Jerusalem duly happened. It was a terrible event for the Jewish people, as Psalm 137 shows. The next temple in Jerusalem was built in the time of Ezra and Nehemiah and stood for over 500 years. It was replaced by another temple (the "second" temple) built by King Herod and this was destroyed in A.D.70. It was this last temple whose destruction Jesus prophesied.

The destruction of these temples was so appalling because it threw into question everything that God had revealed to his people.

The Jewish religion was based on the promised presence of God in his temple. Yet he says that they should not trust in the deceptive words, "the temple of the Lord, the temple of the Lord". The temple would not save them from the judgement of their sin. Worse, he would remove his presence because of their appalling behaviour. They lied, worshipped false gods, shed innocent blood in the temple itself, dealt unjustly, committed adultery, oppressed: the list seems endless. God's promises were conditional on their behaviour, and they failed. The temple would not save them. They would not be safe from destruction in the temple.

From the promised presence of God in his temple flowed the whole structure of Jewish life. Here they made sacrifices so that they could be forgiven by God and live. Here the priesthood, the intercessors between God and the people, performed their essential tasks. Here was the place of the great festivals which gathered the people together and made them one. Here was the whole prestige and honour of the people.

The destruction of the temple was much, much more than a closure of a church, however beautiful and important. Without the temple there was no hope, no future, no forgiveness, no unity, no life. It showed that God had judged them and had left them. The destruction of Solomon's temple by the Babylonians in B.C. 587 was the greatest tragedy in the history of the Jewish people up to that point.

All of this puts into perspective the prophetic action of Jesus in the temple. In our study of the temple, every one of Jesus' actions and words about the temple are of great importance, but none more so than his judgement of the temple which is reported in all four gospels. Jesus quotes Jeremiah directly with the words of judgement he used, "a den of robbers".

His actions as well as his words in the temple are equally prophetic. The sweeping away of the money changers is more than just a protest against business practices going on in the temple. It is true that the money changers were cheating the people by giving them poor rates, the same kind of oppression against the poor and widows as was happening in Jeremiah's time. More importantly they were handling Roman coinage, the denarius, which carried the head of Caesar and included the words, "divine Caesar" on the side. To devout Jews this was the same as acknowledging a false god. At the same time the temple authorities were hand-in-glove with the oppressive Romans.

Jesus' release of the animals and the doves was another prophetic action. Jesus was enacting the end of the sacrificial system in the temple. Without animals, there could be no sacrifice, and without sacrifices, there could be no forgiveness.

Of course, all this was symbolic. Within a few minutes the traders would have set up again, no doubt angry and bemused at their discomfort. Yet at the same time it was deadly serious. Jesus had also spoken of the destruction of the temple and (twisted by the false witnesses) appeared to believe he was able to destroy the temple and rebuild it in three days! Both claims seemed laughably impossible. In fact they were claims of the greatest divine power: to be able to destroy the very place where God lived, and to be able to build it again.

The stakes were the highest. Was Jesus a genuine prophet, a second Jeremiah, pronouncing the judgement of God and even more? Or was he a false prophet, one who was disturbing the peace of Jerusalem? The authorities took the same view as they did with Jeremiah, the only difference being that Jesus was executed and Jeremiah escaped.

Yet in AD 70 the destruction came. The behaviour at that time, if the historian Josephus is to be believed, was at least as bad as at the time as Jeremiah, and the consequences were similar. A foreign, pagan army desecrated and destroyed the temple. The people were scattered and eventually exiled from Jerusalem altogether. Jesus prophecy was as true as that of Jeremiah.

The result for the Jewish people was equally traumatic. All the horrors of the loss of the temple were there. What were they to do? There were two different solutions by the Jewish people. The first eventually became what we now call Judaism. They reorganised themselves around the synagogues, which was a relatively new idea at the time. The temple and Jerusalem were no longer essential, and the law of Moses became the most important part of the religion. The memory remained, and many hoped that the temple would be rebuilt, but in the short term it was not necessary. This was the triumph of what had been the Pharisaical party in Jesus' time, against other groups like the Sadducees and the Zealots.

The second response was what we now call Christianity. The Jewish followers of Jesus, and the also his new Gentile followers, had no need for the temple. Jesus had predicted its destruction, and had also predicted that it would be raised in three days. Every Christian knew that Jesus had replaced the temple in a fundamental way. All those things that the temple meant to the Jews—a hope, a future, forgiveness, unity, life—all of this was now in the resurrected Messiah. He had fulfilled everything. Thus Judaism split, between those who recognised the temple in their midst, and those who lived without it and hoped for it to be rebuilt in the distant future.

As followers of Jesus we are in the second group, those for whom the temple takes on a completely new meaning. In fact, the promise of the temple has been fulfilled in the most wonderful way, as Jesus fulfils all the promises of the Old Covenant (2 Corinthians. 1:20). However it is still necessary that we too take on board the warning of the destruction of the temple made with stone. Are we too sometimes those who say, "The temple of the Lord, the temple of the Lord"? Do we too put our trust in the temple in a way that is false?

We may say that our trust is in Christ, but do our actions match our words? As Christians are we too sucked into the prevailing culture as the Israelites of old had been, to worship false gods? Or do we simply not obey the commands of Christ, desiring our own ends? Jesus himself says, "Not everyone who says to me, 'Lord, Lord', will enter the kingdom of heaven, but only he who does the will of my Father, who is in heaven." (Matthew 7:21)

There is another side to those who trusted in the temple. It had become an element of magic, which would protect them from all ills and the consequences of all their actions. It can be true for us as Christians as well. We expect the miracles of the risen Christ to happen in our lives, not appreciating that there are times when we are called to share in the suffering of Christ, or of our neighbours, or in suffering that is a direct consequence of our actions. The grace of Christ is a gift, not a magic potion for all who say "Lord, Lord".

The destruction of the temple is a warning for all of us who call ourselves Christians and who trust in a wrong way in Christ. The time comes when it is necessary to bow the knee to the one we call Lord, and follow his way, if necessary to Calvary.

## Questions to consider
What does the Lordship of Jesus mean to you?
What do you trust Jesus for?
Are you like those who trusted in the temple?

# 14. The Priest of the Temple

*Psalm 110:1-4*

¹*The LORD says to my Lord: "Sit at my right hand until I make your enemies a footstool for your feet." ²The LORD will extend your mighty sceptre from Zion; you will rule in the midst of your enemies.*

³*Your troops will be willing on your day of battle. Arrayed in holy majesty, from the womb of the dawn you will receive the dew of your youth. ⁴The LORD has sworn and will not change his mind: "You are a priest for ever, in the order of Melchizedek."*

*Matthew 22:42-46*

*[Jesus asked the Pharisees]:* ⁴²*"What do you think about the Christ? Whose son is he?" "The son of David," they replied.* ⁴³*He said to them, "How is it then that David, speaking by the Spirit, calls him 'Lord'? For he says,* ⁴⁴*" 'The Lord said to my Lord: "Sit at my right hand until I put your enemies under your feet." '* ⁴⁵*If then David calls him 'Lord,' how can he be his son?"* ⁴⁶*No-one could say a word in reply, and from that day on no-one dared to ask him any more questions.*

*Hebrews 7:17, 21-28*

¹⁷*It is declared: "You are a priest for ever, in the order of Melchizedek... the Lord has sworn and will not change his mind: 'You are a priest for ever.' "* ²²*Because of this oath, Jesus has become the guarantee of a better covenant.* ²³*Now there have been many of those priests, since death prevented them from continuing in office;* ²⁴*but because Jesus lives for ever, he has a permanent priesthood.* ²⁵*Therefore he is able to save completely those who come to God through him, because he always lives to intercede for them.* ²⁶*Such a high priest meets our need—one who is holy, blameless, pure, set apart from sinners, exalted above the heavens.* ²⁷*Unlike*

the other high priests, he does not need to offer sacrifices day after day, first for his own sins, and then for the sins of the people. He sacrificed for their sins once for all when he offered himself. $^{28}$For the law appoints as high priests men who are weak; but the oath, which came after the law, appointed the Son, who has been made perfect for ever.

*Genesis 14:18-20*
$^{18}$*Then Melchizedek king of Salem brought out bread and wine. He was priest of God Most High, $^{19}$and he blessed Abram, saying, "Blessed be Abram by God Most High, Creator of heaven and earth. $^{20}$And blessed be God Most High, who delivered your enemies into your hand." Then Abram gave him a tenth of everything.*

There are times when the first line or the first verse of a song or poem automatically reminds us of the whole song or poem. For example,

"Humpty Dumpty sat on a wall,
 Humpty Dumpty had a great fall,"
 What comes next?

Or perhaps, less trivially,
"Away in a manger,
 no crib for a bed,"

We live in a culture where less and less is committed to memory but even us, if we sing a song often enough, know that it becomes ingrained in our very being. I know that this is especially true of well-loved hymns.

When Jesus was speaking to the Pharisees in Matthew 22 it was in the last week before the crucifixion. He was standing in the temple in Jerusalem itself, openly entering into controversy and dispute with the religious leaders. He had just contradicted the powerful Sadducees about the resurrection, and now he challenges the Pharisees. Jesus asks them what they think about the Messiah, specifically asking whose son he is. They reply that he is David's son, but Jesus corrects them, quoting Psalm 110, by saying he is David's Lord.

This seems an opaque and sterile argument for us today, and we often move quickly on to Jesus' straightforward attack on the hypocrisy of the Pharisees in Matthew 23. However Jesus' quotation of Psalm 110 is very significant, not least because all of those listening would have known the whole Psalm by heart. It was sung regularly and as familiar to his hearers as "Away in a manger" is to us. To extend the example further, if we sung "Away in a manger" on Christmas Eve, no-one would think twice. If we sung it in mid-February, in a service for the homeless, everyone's mind would immediately go to "no crib for a bed" and "asleep on the hay". Jesus does something similarly provocative: he quotes the psalm in the temple. Psalm 110 is a Messianic psalm and everyone knew that it was to the temple that the Messiah would come. Many hoped or feared that Jesus would announce himself as Messiah, and now here he is quoting Psalm 110. Jesus was increasing the tension.

Psalm 110 speaks of one greater than king David ruling in great power and majesty, and it speaks of him being a priest for ever, in the order of Melchizedek. By using this quotation Jesus was not denying that the Messiah was of the house of David; rather he was asserting that the Messiah was also recognised by David in his psalm as also being greater that the greatest king of Israel. Why is this so confrontational? Simply this: if Jesus was about to announce unambiguously that he was the Messiah, then he was also saying that he was greater than David. He was saying that he was a priest after the order of Melchizedek. He was saying that he was the authority over the temple and both anointed king and High Priest. In short, he had just raised the stakes a further level. If he were to announce that he was the Messiah, the whole of the religious order of the Jewish people was being threatened. They didn't dare ask any more questions but they plotted his death fearing an unambiguous announcement.

This perhaps does not seem so strange to Christians today, weaned on the New Testament writings that make it plain that our Lord was indeed Messiah and did indeed begin a new covenant.

But that is to look back with hindsight. At the time, his comments meant the shaking of the very foundations for his hearers.

The problem is that we easily miss it, because we do not know Psalm 110 as they did. Jesus only quoted one verse. Yet the writer to the Hebrews had no doubt, also quoting Psalm 110 and spelling out the meaning in detail. Jesus is speaking of kingship and priesthood, and because we are looking at the temple, let us concentrate on the priesthood aspect.

The priestly caste in the temple were of the greatest importance, from the High Priest down to the those who, like Zechariah, were chosen by lot to occasionally lead some part of the worship. They were a powerful elite, essential for worship and especially for the sacrifices. They were set apart by God for this task at the inauguration of the tabernacle. In this one reference, Jesus is putting the whole of the temple worship under threat.

Melchizedek was the king of Salem (Jerusalem) and priest of the Most High God in Genesis 14:18-20 who brought bread and wine to Abraham after he had defeated the kings who had captured Lot. He blessed Abraham and Abraham gave a tenth of all he had captured. There are a number of significant attributes to Melchizedek that the writer to the Hebrews is keen to point out and which were also debated by the scholars in Jesus' time. By using this Psalm, the Pharisees at the very least knew the direction at which Jesus was driving.

Firstly, Melchizedek was greater than Abraham, because he blessed him. Abraham acknowledged this by giving a tithe. Second, Melchizedek was prior to the Levitical priesthood in the temple. He was not bound by the regulations. In particular, he did not descend from Aaron, as all priests had to. Likewise, Jesus descended from Judah, not Levi. Thirdly, Melchizedek had no known beginning or ending, like Jesus. Only an eternal priest can effect an eternal salvation.

All of this means that Jesus, who had already revealed his

Messiahship to his disciples, was claiming to be the great High Priest following the example of Melchizedek. In this one short dispute he is implying, for those with ears to hear, that the need for priests was about to end. We have already looked at his prediction of the destruction of the temple. We shall see later that he is also the sacrifice itself. Jesus then is, in himself, fulfilling all that the temple was doing. He is fulfilling the law and bringing about a new covenant.

What did a priest do? Why was he so needed? We have seen (chapter 10) that the role of the High priest was to offer sacrifices, above all on the Day of Atonement. "Aaron is to offer the bull for his own sin offering to make atonement for himself and his household" (Leviticus 16:6). This was followed by the sacrifice of a goat as a sin offering and the release of another as a scapegoat (Leviticus 16). The High Priest also offered many other sacrifices. However Jesus had no need to offer any sacrifice on his own behalf, because he was sinless. Rather, he offered up a sacrifice for atonement as a High Priest should. He himself said, "The Son of Man came to give his life as a ransom for many" (Mark 10:45) and his blood was "poured out for many" (Mark 14:24). He knew that he was going to act as a true High Priest, but more, that his offering was going to be the final and complete sacrifice that did away with the need for any more sacrifices to be offered.

Secondly, a High Priest existed to make intercessions to God, as the intermediary of the people. "I have prayed for you" he says to Simon Peter at the Last Supper. In John 17 his great prayer, on the same night before offering his sacrifice, has become known as the "High Priestly" prayer. Yet our Lord's position before the Father now is not that he is pleading before the Father. His ascension showed that he is now the great Priest-King, enthroned in glory. Surely it is his whole glorified life at the right-hand of the Father that is his prayer. His offering is wholly acceptable and wholly effective, and therefore his priestly-ministry on our behalf is never ending. The salvation he secured is absolute.

Thirdly, a priest gives blessing, as did Melchizedek. "Peace be with you", says the risen Jesus. "Blessed are those who have not seen and yet believed" (John 20). Still from heaven Jesus blesses his people.

Jesus little quote from Psalm 110 goes much further and much deeper than it appears at first sight. It interlocks with his other statements: he was the fulfilment of all the High Priests down the ages. He was the priest after the order of Melchizedek.

## Questions to consider

Ponder Jesus offering of himself on the cross.
What does it mean to be both offering and offerer?
What difference does Jesus' blessing and intercession make in everyday life?
In what sense can there be priesthood on earth today?

# 15. The Water from the Temple

*Ezekiel 47:1-12*

<sup>1</sup>*The man brought me back to the entrance of the temple, and I saw water coming out from under the threshold of the temple towards the east (for the temple faced east). The water was coming down from under the south side of the temple, south of the altar.* <sup>2</sup>*He then brought me out through the north gate and led me round the outside to the outer gate facing east, and the water was flowing from the south side.* <sup>3</sup>*As the man went eastward with a measuring line in his hand, he measured off a thousand cubits and then led me through water that was ankle-deep.* <sup>4</sup>*He measured off another thousand cubits and led me through water that was knee-deep. He measured off another thousand and led me through water that was up to the waist.* <sup>5</sup>*He measured off another thousand, but now it was a river that I could not cross, because the water had risen and was deep enough to swim in—a river that no-one could cross.* <sup>6</sup>*He asked me, "Son of man, do you see this?"*

*Then he led me back to the bank of the river.* <sup>7</sup>*When I arrived there, I saw a great number of trees on each side of the river.* <sup>8</sup>*He said to me, "This water flows towards the eastern region and goes down into the Arabah, where it enters the Sea. When it empties into the Sea, the water there becomes fresh.* <sup>9</sup>*Swarms of living creatures will live wherever the river flows. There will be large numbers of fish, because this water flows there and makes the salt water fresh; so where the river flows everything will live.* <sup>10</sup>*Fishermen will stand along the shore; from En Gedi to En Eglaim there will be places for spreading nets. The fish will be of many kinds— like the fish of the Great Sea.* <sup>11</sup>*But the swamps and marshes will not become fresh; they will be left for salt.* <sup>12</sup>*Fruit trees of all kinds will grow on both banks of the river. Their leaves will not wither, nor will their fruit fail. Every month they will bear, because the water from the sanctuary flows to them. Their fruit will serve for food and their leaves for healing."*

*John 7:37-39*

*[37]On the last and greatest day of the Feast, Jesus stood and said in a loud voice, "If anyone is thirsty, let him come to me and drink. [38]Whoever believes in me, as the Scripture has said, streams of living water will flow from within him." [39]By this he meant the Spirit, whom those who believed in him were later to receive. Up to that time the Spirit had not been given, since Jesus had not yet been glorified.*

*Revelation 22:1-3*

*[1]Then the angel showed me the river of the water of life, as clear as crystal, flowing from the throne of God and of the Lamb [2]down the middle of the great street of the city. On each side of the river stood the tree of life...and the leaves of the tree are for the healing of the nations. [3]No longer will there be any curse.*

*Genesis 2:8-10*

*[8]Now the LORD God had planted a garden in the east, in Eden; and there he put the man he had formed. [9]And the LORD God made all kinds of trees grow out of the ground—trees that were pleasing to the eye and good for food. In the middle of the garden were the tree of life and the tree of the knowledge of good and evil. [10]A river watering the garden flowed from Eden; from there it was separated into four headwaters.*

We had planned next day to go to Azraq, the oasis town in the middle of the Jordanian desert. However during the night there were violent thunderstorms over the high hills of Amman that drained east into the desert. Next day the air was fresh and clear, the spring sun shone and the world was newly washed. But as we headed east the wet desert soil started to turn into pools. We crossed a raging torrent that 364 days of the year was as dry as a bone. The river continued on into the desert as far was we could see. Finally, the road itself began to be flooded. The car radio told us that Azraq could not be reached that day.

In the Middle East water has always been the basis of life. In Britain we covet sunshine; there they covet water. They have enough sun and warmth. Life depends on the rains and on the rivers. Yet the waters can be deceptive, dangerous. The salt of the Dead Sea prevented life. The storms of the seas led to death by drowning, even in the Sea of Galilee.

Jesus went to the temple at the Feast of Tabernacles. The feast was one of the three great pilgrimage festivals of the year (with Passover and Pentecost) and celebrated the ingathering of the harvest. For seven days everyone lived outside in "tabernacles" or booths made from branches, which reminded them of the wandering time of the Exodus. Although the feast is laid down in the Torah (Exodus 23:16) the ceremony of water pouring was a later addition. It recognised rain as a gift from God, needed for good harvests. It also looked back to God's provision of water in the desert (Exodus 17:1-7). Carson[1] describes what happened as follows:

"On the seven days of the Feast of Tabernacles, a golden flagon was filled with water from the pool of Siloam and was carried in a procession led by the High Priest back to the temple. As the procession approached the Watergate on the south side of the inner court three blasts from the trumpet were sounded. While the pilgrims watched, the priests processed around the altar with the flagon, the temple choir singing the *Hallel* (Psalms 113-118). When the choir reached Psalm 118, every male pilgrim shook the *lulab* (willow and myrtle twigs tied with palm) in his right hand, while his left raised a piece of citrus fruit (a sign of the ingathered harvest), and all cried "Give thanks to the Lord!" three times. The water was offered to God at the time of morning sacrifice, along with the daily drink offering (of wine)."

Jesus is deliberately associating himself with the great events of the

---

[1] D. A. Carson, *The Gospel According to John*, Apollos 1991 p.322

feast in the temple. He says, "Come to *me* and drink". He is like the rock in the exodus from which the water flowed for the thirsty people in the desert. However, he says more than this. The water he gives is "living" water, which will spread out from everyone who believes in him. (Notice, incidentally, that he is the original source of the water, not the believer.) The idea of living water occurs in the Old Testament. One of the best examples is Ezekiel's great vision of the temple, from which flowed rivers of living water. This image, in turn, looks back to Genesis and is picked up by John in Revelation.

According to Ezekiel's vision the water will pour out from the altar of the temple itself. The water will deepen rapidly as it flows a little like the river I saw that day in the desert. However this river is quite unnatural. Within 4000 cubits (1800 metres) it became a river so deep that no-one could cross it. Usually rivers slowly build in volume and depth, with many tributaries contributing. Even a desert flash flood only rises that quickly for a short time, and then from very steep gullies. Here we have a sudden upwelling of water from one source that becomes an overwhelming, permanent river.

This water is special in another way as well. It is the source of life to the land and sea, not only to the desert but the Dead Sea. The Dead Sea is a great expanse of very salty water that kills all life. There is a Byzantine map of the Holy Land in the form of a mosaic, known as the Madaba map from the Jordanian town where it was made. The map is a remarkable artistic achievement in itself and the oldest depiction of Jerusalem in existence. However in one small corner the map shows a charming detail. It shows fish swimming down the Jordan River towards the Dead Sea, but where the river enters the sea there is a fish swimming in the other direction, away from the death that awaits it. The river of life flowing from the altar of the temple transforms the desert and it also reverses the death of the Dead Sea into life. The sea will teem with as much fish life as the Mediterranean, so that fishermen can earn their living all the way along the banks of the sea.

Meanwhile the trees beside the river are not natural trees either. They will fruit every month, their leaves will not wither. They are unmistakably similar to the trees in the Garden of Eden, and the book of Revelation uses almost identical language. We have here a vision of the future when God will complete all things and put all things right.

Jesus was connecting with these images when he spoke of himself as the source of living water. He was speaking in the temple precinct, calling out in a loud voice so that all could hear. He was replacing the water rite in the temple, and we have here another example of how he was fulfilling everything promised in the Old Covenant. He is the rock from which the water sprang, he is the fulfilment of all they were doing, he was and is the beginning of life. The Jews believed that the temple is the source of life. They knew that it was the dwelling place of God, and it was here that it was possible to receive true life. But they had not responded to the great change. God was among them, and he came and went from the temple in his daily life. God had come to them in a new form, in the form of a man, and they could not recognise him. He spoke in the temple in a loud voice, saying he was the source of the living water, but they wondered and, in the main, did not accept. They had the wrong temple, and the wrong idea of life.

The new life began with death. The fulfilment of Ezekiel's prophecy came at the crucifixion when water flowed from Jesus' side. It flowed in a trickle to begin with but it became an overwhelming flood. It has flowed so deep and strong that those spiritually dead (as dead as the Dead Sea) can receive everlasting life. Therefore in John's vision we see the permanent fate of God's people: to live in the land of healing and life. This is why streams of living water can flow from whoever believes in Jesus. Those who once were dead, become alive, and more than alive, the source of life like their saviour. If the Dead Sea can provide life previously the dead people can give life as well.

The image goes even further. John tells us that the water Jesus gave is the Spirit of Life himself, that aspect of God we call the Holy Spirit. In Genesis 1:2 we read that the Spirit of God was hovering over the waters, the waters of chaos before God made them the waters of life. It is the work of the Holy Spirit that brings this new life. Our reception of the Holy Spirit when we first commit ourselves to Jesus is the beginning of the new creation of life within us.

John's Gospel tells us a number of times about the Holy Spirit. The incident of Nicodemus visiting Jesus (in John 3) also happened at the time of a great feast, this time Passover, and Jesus was certainly in the vicinity of the temple after his actions in John 2. Here he speaks of the Holy Spirit giving new birth, new life to the recipient. The Spirit is a wind, blowing where he will. In John 7 the Spirit is water, flowing and overwhelming and transforming. The image of God transforming those first disciples, and us, and eventually the whole world, is varied because it has to be.

There is no one way of describing the Spirit of the living God. However the image of water as the giver of life coming from the temple is one found in many places in scripture. Jesus is saying that he is the fulfilment of the promise of the temple. He is the source of that water, as he is the giver and that he is generous with it beyond our understanding. What must we do? We must come to him, and we must believe in him. It is astonishingly simple. He promises to quench our thirst, and give us an abundance of life such that there will be water or life for all. All we need to do is to come to him and believe.

## Questions to consider

What does it mean to come to Jesus? How can we do it ourselves?

Can you see how you have been the source of life for others?

How does the vision of new life from Ezekiel affect you?

How would you translate it into modern life?

# 16. The Light in the Temple

*Exodus 13:21-22*

*²¹By day the LORD went ahead of them in a pillar of cloud to guide them on their way and by night in a pillar of fire to give them light, so that they could travel by day or night. ²²Neither the pillar of cloud by day nor the pillar of fire by night left its place in front of the people.*

*Exodus 40:34-35*

*³⁴Then the cloud covered the Tent of Meeting, and the glory of the LORD filled the tabernacle. ³⁵Moses could not enter the Tent of Meeting because the cloud had settled upon it, and the glory of the LORD filled the tabernacle.*

*Exodus 27:20-21*

*²⁰"Command the Israelites to bring you clear oil of pressed olives for the light so that the lamps may be kept burning. ²¹In the Tent of Meeting, outside the curtain that is in front of the Testimony, Aaron and his sons are to keep the lamps burning before the LORD from evening till morning. This is to be a lasting ordinance among the Israelites for the generations to come".*

*John 7:37; 8:12; 18-27; 33-36*

*³⁷On the last and greatest day of the Feast, Jesus stood and said in a loud voice, "If anyone is thirsty, let him come to me and drink...¹²When Jesus spoke again to the people, he said, "I am the light of the world. Whoever follows me will never walk in darkness, but will have the light of life." ¹⁸I am one who testifies for myself; my other witness is the Father, who sent me." ¹⁹Then they asked him, "Where is your father?" "You do not know me or my Father," Jesus replied. "If you knew me, you would know my Father also." ²⁰He spoke these words while teaching in the temple area near the place where* the offerings were put. Yet no-one seized him, because his time had not yet come. ²¹Once more Jesus said to them, "I am going away, and you will look for me, and you will die in your sin. Where I go, you cannot come." ²²This made the Jews ask, "Will he kill himself? Is that why he says, 'Where I go, you cannot come'?" ²³But he continued, "You are from below; I am from above. You are of this world; I am not of this world. ²⁴I told you that you would die in your sins; if you do not believe that I am the one I claim to be, you will indeed die in your sins." ²⁵"Who are you?" they asked. "Just what I have been claiming all along," Jesus replied. ²⁶"I have much to say in judgment of you. But he who sent me is reliable, and what I have heard from him I tell the world." ²⁷They did not understand that he was telling them about his Father.

³³They answered him, "We are Abraham's descendants and have never been slaves of anyone. How can you say that we shall be set free?" ³⁴Jesus replied, "I tell you the truth, everyone who sins is a slave to sin. ³⁵Now a slave has no permanent place in the family, but a son belongs to it for ever. ³⁶So if the Son sets you free, you will be free indeed..."

One day in Jerusalem I went to the Church of the Holy Sepulchre. In the chapel that is said to be the place of Christ's tomb I found Father Simeon lighting the oil lamps. The scene seemed to have come straight out of the Old Testament: the robes, the turban, the beard, the oil and the lamps: all done in a quiet service to God so that light could be provided. The scene is very Greek Orthodox and you can find something similar all over the Eastern Mediterranean. But there, in Jerusalem, on the very site of the death and resurrection of Christ, there was an added potency. The man who said, "I am the light of the world" was still being remembered by the lighting of lamps, just as they used to do in the tabernacle and in the temple.

When Jesus said, "I am the light of the world", in St. John's gospel, it was still the Feast of Tabernacles, following on from the account in John 7. (Most scholars believe that the first part of John chapter 8 is misplaced, and this is Jesus' second "I am" pronouncement within a short space of time.) Thus he was on the

Temple Mount, speaking of light after speaking about rivers of living water. Both are temple themes, both go to the heart of God in the Old Testament.

There is a fascinating description in rabbinic writing of the lighting of four great lamps in the temple. Although the description is for the first day of the feast, it is understood from other references that it happened each day. We can assume that Jesus saw this as he was in the temple. "Towards the end of the first day of the feast of Tabernacles, people went down into the court of the women, where precautions were taken (to separate the men and the women). Golden lamps were there, and four golden bowls were on each of them, and four ladders were by each; four young men from the priestly group of youths had jugs of oil containing about 120 logs and poured oil from them into the individual bowls. Wicks were made from the discarded trousers of the priests and from their girdles. There was no court in Jerusalem that was not bright from the light…"[1]

The symbol of light was present to all those who were worshipping in the temple and Jesus' words had that specific object. We are so used to the idea of light as a religious theme today that we assume we know what it means. The giving of light, the dawning of the sun, seeing for the first time, enlightenment; all these we quickly imagine when we think of spiritual light. And indeed this is true in part for what Jesus was saying as well. We see it in the events after he said, "I am the light of the world". After his pronouncement he gets into such an argument that he has to leave the temple to save his life from stoning. On his departure he meets the man born blind and heals him secretly, and another controversy erupts over this healing (it takes up the whole of chapter 9). Yet a simple healing would not cause such a dispute. It is because of his words earlier in the temple that the healing is so controversial, and because of his repetition of, "I am the light of the world" (John 9:5). So what was this dispute?

When he says, "I am the light of the world", he says it in a

[1] from *Sukkh.* 5.1, as quoted in G. Beasley-Murray, 'John', Word Biblical Commentary, 36, 1987 p.127

specific place with a short commentary. "Whoever follows me will never walk in darkness, but will have the light of life." This immediately had significance for the worshippers in the temple. They were coming to celebrate their release from Egypt, from the captivity of Pharaoh all the centuries previously. When they escaped they were led by a pillar of cloud by day and a pillar of fire by night. The pillar of fire gave them light so that they could travel in the darkness (Exodus 13:21). This was the glory of the living God that went before them, and this same glory descended on the temple. His glory, his light, also descended on Solomon's temple. In short, Jesus' words are a deliberate echoing of the words from the Exodus. He is the light, he brings salvation, he provides the leadership in the darkness to the Promised Land, he brings light to the world and, by very strong implication, he is the light in the temple. These are the primary themes of spiritual light that he claims. Let us look at each of these in turn.

*1. The Lord is my light and my salvation (Psalm 27:1)*

Jesus' words were powerful stuff for those Jews, and it is for us today. Jesus is saying that he is the leader out of bondage and slavery, not as a second Moses, but as God himself. When he says, in another "I am" that he is the way, the truth and the life, he is saying something very similar. The first century Jews were steeped in the history of Israel, of the actions of their God. They were looking for God to act to save them out of the slavery of the present occupation, so that they could lead a life unpolluted and pleasing to God. Yet Jesus is consistently challenging this diagnosis. Yes, indeed, they need salvation, but it is not the Romans who are the main problem, but their own hearts. So the Pharisees challenge him, not on his statement, but in his authority to make it in the first place. Jesus' replies in John 8 are very provocative. He says to them that he stands with the Father (v.16); that the Father is his witness (v.18); that they do not know the Father (v.19); that they are worldly and will die in their sins (v.23,24); and that they will lift up the Son of Man (v.27). Jesus knew his death was simultaneously the rising of the Son of Man in glory to the Father that was predicted in Daniel. Still they question him, claiming to be free, because they are sons of Abraham (v.33). His reply is stunning: they are slaves to sin, and they need the Son to set them free (v.34-36). All this takes place in the temple (v.20), in the light of the temple lamps.

### 2. Your word is a lamp for my feet and a light for my path (Psalm 119:105)

All of this is a return to the Exodus theme of the need for deliverance. The light is the way to salvation. Here we see the second element of the light: the beacon leading us on. He leads us to salvation, as God led the Israelites through the desert. They had been saved through the waters of the Red Sea, but they still had some way to go before they reached the Promised Land. We are in exactly that place today, if we have already trusted in the Son of Man lifted high. He is the light in the darkness, showing us where to go in our lives. We can choose to disobey, as they did frequently in the desert, with dire consequences, or we can choose to be sensible and follow. If we do, Jesus will go ahead.

### 3. I will also make you a light for the Gentiles, that you bring salvation to the ends of the earth (Isaiah 49:6)

One of the great points of controversy centres on exactly who the people of salvation are. It is obvious in the discussion between Jesus and the Pharisees that being children of Abraham was of the greatest importance. But Jesus draws a distinction between being Abraham's descendants (v.37) who are ready to kill him, and Abraham's children (v.39) who do not do such things. This reaches its climax in his announcement, "Before Abraham was born, I am", for which they wanted to stone him. Jesus is before and higher than Abraham. Thus when he says he is the light of the world, it is no small claim. It is the fulfilment of Isaiah 49, that the promise of God has gone beyond the descendants of Abraham to the Gentiles, who can become his children. Jesus is the light for the Gentiles. The Pharisees taught that Israel was to be the light for the Gentiles; Jesus taught differently, that he is the promised light. Jesus then can be our light, whatever our background. This was a horrific thought to the pious Pharisees he was speaking to. It is a repetition of John the Baptist's claim that God can make children of Abraham from the stones. All this is comforting to us if we are Christians today, but I wonder whether it should be. Where is God working today? Is it only among those who claim to be Christians? Are we, to use the comparison, children of Jesus, or only descendants by human birth? Are we outraged when we see God work with those we might see as sinful Christians? The Pharisees would have seen the blind man as sinful and rejected by God. Are we upset if we see Christ working today with people of other religions? Do we forget how he dealt with the Roman centurion? Are we better?

*4. Then the Lord my God will come (to Jerusalem), and all the holy ones with him. On that day there will be no light, no cold or frost. It will be a unique day, without daytime or night-time—a day known to the Lord. When evening comes, there will be light. (Zechariah 14:5-7).*

Jesus came to the temple as the light of the world. No longer is the temple the only place to find the light of God, his glory. The light is now spread abroad. This is the beginning of The Day, which will be completed when Jesus returns. In the meantime, Greek Orthodox clergy like Father Simeon do not light lamps in imitation of the temple, but as a reminder that Christ has replaced it, and that his church is everywhere, wherever he reigns in human hearts.

## Questions to consider

How do we accept Jesus helping those we think are sinners or non-Christians?

How does the light of Jesus lead us day by day?

How well do you remember how Jesus led you into freedom from sin?

Could you describe it in words?

# 17. The Sacrifice in the Temple

*Genesis 22: 2, 13-14*

²*Then God said, "Take your son, your only son, Isaac, whom you love, and go to the region of Moriah. Sacrifice him there as a burnt offering on one of the mountains I will tell you about." *¹³*Abraham looked up and there in a thicket he saw a ram caught by its horns. He went over and took the ram and sacrificed it as a burnt offering instead of his son. *¹⁴*So Abraham called that place The Lord Will Provide. And to this day it is said, "On the mountain of the Lord it will be provided."*

*Deuteronomy 16:2-7*

²*Sacrifice as the Passover to the Lord your God an animal from your flock or herd at the place the Lord will choose as a dwelling for his Name. *³*Do not eat it with bread made with yeast, but for seven days eat unleavened bread, the bread of affliction, because you left Egypt in haste—so that all the days of your life you may remember the time of your departure from Egypt. *⁴*Let no yeast be found in your possession in all your land for seven days. Do not let any of the meat you sacrifice on the evening of the first day remain until morning. *⁵*You must not sacrifice the Passover in any town the Lord your God gives you *⁶*except in the place he will choose as a dwelling for his Name. There you must sacrifice the Passover in the evening, when the sun goes down, on the anniversary of your departure from Egypt. *⁷*Roast it and eat it at the place the Lord your God will choose.*

*2 Chronicles 35:1-2*

¹*Josiah celebrated the Passover to the Lord in Jerusalem, and the Passover lamb was slaughtered on the fourteenth day of the first month. *²*He appointed the priests to their duties and encouraged them in the service of the Lord's temple.*

*The Temple*

*Isaiah 53:7*

> [7]*He was led like a lamb to the slaughter.*

*John 1:29*

> [29]*The next day John saw Jesus coming towards him and said, "Look, the Lamb of God, who takes away the sin of the world!"*

*Luke 22:7-8, 13-20*

> [7]*Then came the day of Unleavened Bread on which the Passover lamb had to be sacrificed.* [8]*Jesus sent Peter and John, saying, "Go and make preparations for us to eat the Passover." So they prepared the Passover.* [14]*When the hour came, Jesus and his apostles reclined at the table.* [15]*And he said to them, "I have eagerly desired to eat this Passover with you before I suffer.* [16]*For I tell you, I will not eat it again until it finds fulfilment in the kingdom of God."* [17]*After taking the cup, he gave thanks and said, "Take this and divide it among you.* [18]*For I tell you I will not drink again of the fruit of the vine until the kingdom of God comes."* [19]*And he took bread, gave thanks and broke it, and gave it to them, saying, "This is my body given for you; do this in remembrance of me."* [20]*In the same way, after the supper he took the cup, saying, "This cup is the new covenant in my blood, which is poured out for you".*

*1 Corinthians 5:7*

> *Christ, our Passover Lamb, has been sacrificed.*

*Revelation 21:22*

> [22]*I did not see a temple in the city, because the Lord God Almighty and the Lamb are its temple.*

When I first lived in Jordan the father of a colleague of mine, a bank manger, had a heart attack and was in danger of dying. In fact he was the manager of a branch of the Petra Bank, owned by Ahmed Chalabi. (Dr Chalabi is a very controversial figure. He is a

Shi'ite Iraqi who fled Jordan as a wanted man a little later when the Petra Bank went bankrupt. Later he was supported by the U.S. and after the invasion of Iraq he became deputy Prime Minister.) A little later my colleague's father (who was, as it happens, a Christian) recovered and returned home. In thankfulness to God and for his recovery, Chalabi ordered a sheep to be sacrificed on the steps of every Petra Bank in the kingdom. This is the culture of blood sacrifice and it still exists.

The Passover lamb was chosen five days before the sacrifice, which was the day Jesus rode into Jerusalem on a donkey. Each family or group chose a lamb to be sacrificed. It was chosen because it was pure and spotless. On the afternoon before the Passover, at 3 o'clock, the lambs were slaughtered in the court of the temple. A lamb could be killed by laymen, but the blood had to be caught by priests. A priest caught the blood in a golden or silver cup, and when it was full it was passed along a line of priests to the altar, where it was sprinkled. The lamb was then hung up on hooks and skinned. The fatty portions were offered on the altar as a burnt offering. The scene that afternoon would have been, to our eyes, a scene of devastation and extremism so alien that we probably could not have coped. There would have been thousands within the precinct; the priests were singing, the people sacrificing their animals, the stench of live animals and blood and smoke everywhere.

There is controversy about whether the Passover sacrifices the year of Jesus' crucifixion was on the Thursday or Friday. The gospels give, on the face of it, different accounts. Either the disciples celebrated the Passover meal with Jesus and he died the day after the sacrifice, or they celebrated a kind of early Passover, and Jesus was sacrificed at the same time as the animals in the temple. To me, everything points to the latter, but whatever the chronological reality, the theology speaks straightforwardly of Jesus being our Passover lamb that died at the Passover. There are similarities between the events of the Easter weekend and the Passover: Jesus' deliberate choice of Passover as the day of choosing the sacrifice, the fact that Jesus bones were not broken (they couldn't be on the lamb), the eating of the Last Supper within Jerusalem. But there is also a vivid contrast: Jesus died outside the city walls. The Passover had to take place within Jerusalem.

Passover celebrated the release from Egypt, the release from slavery. The ritual of haste in eating and the need to mark with blood all look back to this time. The Passover sacrifice was in Jerusalem itself because of the temple. Abraham led his son up to die on Mount Moriah where Jerusalem was later built. The temple in Jerusalem was where God chose to dwell. Josiah reintroduced the Passover in Jerusalem when the law was rediscovered. Here was the place to remember the deliverance from Egypt by the Passover sacrifice. Once again we find that the important things in the life of Jesus are tied in with the temple. It is an essential part of the salvation story.

Jesus chose to celebrate the Passover before his death with his disciples. When he did so he deliberately began a new rite. He says, "Do this in remembrance of me". What happened that evening he did not intend to be forgotten. It was to be remembered in just the same way that the Passover was remembered by a sacred ceremony. The Last Supper is one of only two new religious ceremonies commanded by our Lord (the other is baptism). It is of the highest importance. What does it mean? "This is my body, which is given for you." The Passover sacrifices happened every year; the body of the lamb was consumed each year, while its blood was sprinkled on the altar each year. "This cup is the new covenant in my blood, which is poured out for you." When he died his blood was poured out, our Passover sacrifice. There is to be no more blood sacrifice. It is very significant that there is no mention of a lamb in the Last Supper; Jesus himself is the lamb. In fact we can go further: now the lamb is the temple itself, as John saw in his vision.

So Jesus is actually replacing the Passover feast. That was something the disciples could not understand until later. But our Lord knew what he was doing. With the crucifixion the Passover was being fulfilled. It is no longer necessary for us to bring a lamb for a

physical sacrifice. It is no longer necessary for us to sprinkle blood. Instead he did something very different. He gave us something to remember that looked back to the last Passover. He gave us a new covenant in his blood.

These words are so familiar to us today that it is easy for us to miss the full meaning of them. Jesus, in this simple supper, was doing everything the religious hierarchy of his time feared. He was replacing the very basis of the Jewish faith. He is the fulfilment in such a surprising way that it is still not acceptable to good Jews. The use of the word "covenant" (Luke 22:30) is no light matter. Covenant is promise, and in this context it means the promises of God himself to his people. To proclaim a new covenant is to add to those promises. In fact it is to do more: it is to fulfil them, and in that way replace them. The old promises are not dead; rather they are transformed in the person of Jesus into something bigger, better, unexpected and wholly astonishing. Primary among them is the basis for salvation.

How does the Last Supper bring about salvation? The symbolism is all in the temple ceremony occurring at that time. God would pass over the iniquities of those who sacrifice their lamb and sprinkle the blood. The punishment that fell upon the Egyptians did not fall on them. Then God led them out through the waters of death in the Red Sea towards the Promised Land. All this is offered in the bread and the wine, the body and blood. Still there is more. It is not enough just to be part of the community that sacrifices the lamb and applies the blood. One must partake oneself. Thus when we remember, as Jesus commanded us to do, we must apply it for ourselves. We need to partake of the bread and wine, as the first disciples did, and as, in effect, the people of Israel did for centuries until Jesus called them into his fulfilment. How do we do that?

First, we need to come in trust, in faith, that God will do as he promised. Secondly, we need to know that before God we are as undeserving as anyone else. The only difference between them and us is that we are prepared to obey him. Thirdly, our obedience is to trust in the blood, to act for our forgiveness. And fourthly, we consume the sacrifice as a symbol of the effectiveness of what God has done. And finally, Jesus promises to be with us as we do this.

Just as God was in his chosen place, the temple, when the sacrifice was made, so Jesus is with us as we remember his sacrifice on the cross. This is my body, my blood. As we take the memorial of the sacrifice to himself, so he comes to us.

How does he come to us? It is a question upon which books have been written and upon which churches have (tragically) divided, and there is only room here for a brief comment. God came to the Jewish people in the sacrifice of the lamb through the obedience of the people, through his promise to be in the temple and through the actions of the sacrifice. Any suggestion that God was physically present through the eating of the lamb or the sprinkling of the blood would have been anathema. Moreover it does not fit the symbolism of Passover. He was present, but in a way that went beyond the animal. So God in Christ is present today, but in a way that goes beyond the bread and wine. By dying outside the city walls, the Passover and the glory passed from the confines of the temple to all people and all places. Or, to say the same thing another way, the temple, in the form of the lamb who died, is everywhere.

## Questions to consider

What does Holy Communion mean to you?

How do the bread and wine help you to come closer to God?

Why is no lamb mentioned in any of the accounts of the last Supper?

# 18. The Veil of the Temple

*Exodus 26:31-33*

[31]*"Make a curtain of blue, purple and scarlet yarn and finely twisted linen, with cherubim worked into it by a skilled craftsman. [32]Hang it with gold hooks on four posts of acacia wood overlaid with gold and standing on four silver bases. [33]Hang the curtain from the clasps and place the ark of the Testimony behind the curtain. The curtain will separate the Holy Place from the Most Holy Place.*

*Matthew 27:45-54*

[45]*From the sixth hour until the ninth hour darkness came over all the land. [46]About the ninth hour Jesus cried out in a loud voice, "Eloi, Eloi, lama sabachthani?"—which means, "My God, my God, why have you forsaken me?" [47]When some of those standing there heard this, they said, "He's calling Elijah." [48]Immediately one of them ran and got a sponge. He filled it with wine vinegar, put it on a stick, and offered it to Jesus to drink. [49]The rest said, "Now leave him alone. Let's see if Elijah comes to save him." [50]And when Jesus had cried out again in a loud voice, he gave up his spirit. [51]At that moment the curtain of the temple was torn in two from top to bottom. The earth shook and the rocks split. [52]The tombs broke open and the bodies of many holy people who had died were raised to life. [53]They came out of the tombs, and after Jesus' resurrection they went into the holy city and appeared to many people. [54]When the centurion and those with him who were guarding Jesus saw the earthquake and all that had happened, they were terrified, and exclaimed, "Surely he was the Son of God!"*

*Hebrews 10:19-20, 22*

[19]*Therefore, brothers, since we have confidence to enter the Most Holy Place by the blood of Jesus, [20]by a new and living*

*way opened for us through the curtain, that is, his body...* <sup>22</sup>*let us draw near to God*

*2 Corinthians 3:13-16*
<sup>13</sup>*We are not like Moses, who would put a veil over his face to keep the Israelites from gazing at it while the radiance was fading away.* <sup>14</sup>*But their minds were made dull, for to this day the same veil remains when the old covenant is read. It has not been removed, because only in Christ is it taken away.* <sup>15</sup>*Even to this day when Moses is read, a veil covers their hearts.* <sup>16</sup>*But whenever anyone turns to the Lord, the veil is taken away.*

A common sight in many parts of the Middle East is veiled Muslim women. Veiling is not unique to Islam. There is still something similar with nuns in the west today, and in the past in England women wore wimples, a kind of veil over the hair. The veiling of the women is for modesty and also, according to many Muslims, in obedience to the teaching of Islam. The extreme form of the full veil, the hijab, is very controversial today. I have even seen some women driving in a full veil with sunglasses over the top! It was therefore something of a surprise to learn from an Arab woman of what happens when the women are alone at home with their husband or with other women. When the veil comes off underneath all the modest clothing there is often the very latest, sexiest western fashions, certainly among the middle classes. Whatever the given reason for the veil, it is always the case that what lies behind is mysterious simply because it is hidden. A veil is there to hide what lies behind.

Moses face was veiled after he met with God on the mountain, Paul tells us, to prevent the radiance of God reaching the people. The purpose of the veil was the same: to hide something that needs to be hidden. The reason in this case is not modesty or simple obedience (although that is there) but overwhelming glory. Yet in this case, Paul tells us, the veil is taken away in Christ.

Moses needed to be veiled; how much more the Most Holy Place. The Most Holy Place in the tabernacle and the temple was the place where the glory of God resided. It was the place God chose for himself. It was separated from the rest of the temple by a great curtain, a great veil that hung from the ceiling to the floor. This curtain was described in detail in Exodus, and the temple in Jesus' time had a similar curtain, described by the historian Josephus. Speaking of the Sanctuary, the Holy Place, he says: "There were golden doors 82½ feet high and 24 wide. In front of these was a curtain of the same length, Babylonian tapestry embroidered with blue, white linen thread, scarlet and purple, a marvellous example of the craftsman's art. The mixture of materials had a clear mystic meaning, typifying all creation: it seemed the scarlet symbolised fire, linen the earth, blue the air and purple the sea. In two cases the resemblance was one of colour; in the linen and purple it was a question of origin, as the first comes from the earth, the second from the sea. Worked in the tapestry was the whole vista of the heavens except for the signs of the Zodiac." He goes on to say, "The innermost chamber measured 30 feet and was similarly separated by a curtain from the outer part; it was unapproachable, inviolable, and was invisible to all, and was called the Holy of Holies."[1]

The two great curtains in the temple were thus patterned on the original curtains in the tabernacle. Josephus may or may not be right in all his understanding of the symbolism. For example, the purple colour, which came from the murex seashell, may not represent the sea at all, but another aspect of the heavens. What is certain is that the curtains represented the heavens above where God dwelt; the cherubim alone make this apparent, even without "the whole vista of the heavens" to which Josephus alludes. Which of these two veils was torn is not made clear, but the likely answer is the inner veil. Not only is the Greek most often used for the inner curtain, it also makes much more theological sense.

It was at the very moment of the death of Jesus that the veil in the temple was torn in two. The tearing away of the veil must be of the greatest significance, as it is explicitly linked

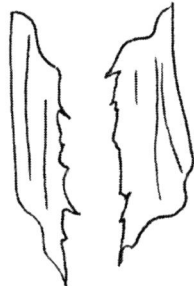

[1] *Josephus, The Jewish War*, v212, Penguin Books 1959, tr. G. A. Williamson

with the moment of death of our Lord. So what is the significance? Actually there are two, although they are closely linked. First, they are important of the physical events associated with the death of Jesus, linked together with the heavenly symbols on the curtain.

When Jesus died, there was a darkening of the sun (Luke 23:44-45), an earthquake, splitting of rocks and the resurrection of believers (although these resurrections were witnessed after Jesus rose, Matthew makes sure we understand that they are to be connected when Jesus died). The symbolism of the colours of the curtain representing the earth and heavens is not mentioned, but it was well known. With the death of Jesus we have events that speak of the death of the old order of creation. Geology, light and physical decay are all set into reverse. To this we need to add the destruction of the temple. The splitting of the veil, together with the rocks, represents the fulfilment that Jesus would destroy the temple and raise it in three days. Without the curtain, the temple is meaningless. There is now open access to the Holy of Holies. The barrier is destroyed, and so is the temple. Thus the old creation begins to be destroyed and the new creation begins. It begins with the resurrection of Jesus, and, if we believe his words, the construction of a new temple. This is the moment of the new creation starting. It makes sense of Jesus' words to the thief on the cross, "today you will be with me in paradise". (Luke 23:43) Paradise in the presence of God is available for those who die in faith.

This leads us on to the second point of the tearing of the veil: a new access to God. The conclusion reached by the writer to the Hebrews is that "we have confidence to enter the Most Holy Place by the blood of Jesus, by a new and living way opened for us for through the curtain, that is, his body". This corresponds accurately to the symbols on the curtain that we are entering the heavenly cosmos. The ripping apart of the curtain means we can enter into the heavenly places into the presence of almighty God himself. The blood shed on the cross by Jesus wins that entry more than the blood of a lamb, and it is permanent. Moreover we no longer need a High Priest to enter the Holy of Holies on our behalf; we can enter through the blood of the Son of God shed for each one of us. He is the one perfect and permanent sacrifice.

There is another essential point about the removal of the veil. If the veil is destroyed, it is not only us who can enter the Holy of Holies. There is movement in the opposite direction. God is released (or rather releases himself) to enter his world. Even though God always was in his world he had limited himself in important ways to his chosen people and to his temple. At that precise moment, when Jesus gave up his spirit on the cross, God releases himself to the world. The Gentile centurion confesses, "Surely he was the Son of God!" The secret is out, the glory is out. The death was outside the city walls, outside the old covenant, yet in the death there is a glory that is beyond anything ever witnessed. The events that follow prove the point. Jesus rises to new life, and ascends to glory in the cloud. He tells them to wait in Jerusalem, and the Holy Spirit is released in wind and fire to the disciples. Jesus tells them to make disciples of all nations, and they find that God himself falls in power on the despised Samaritans and Gentiles. God has come to meet humanity in the fire of his glory.

The destruction of the temple curtain is the climax of the earthly ministry of Jesus, because it corresponds to his death. When it happened, the old order was broken and the new begun. Judgement fell and salvation was revealed. God allowed himself to be approached and poured his Spirit into his world. The temple was destroyed and a new one built. The Son of God had completed his mission.

**Questions to consider**

In what way has a new created order begun?

How do we go to God and how does he come to us today?

Why was it impossible for the veil to remain complete when Jesus died?

# 19. The Temple among us

*Genesis 28:10-19*

[10]*Jacob left Beersheba and set out for Haran.* [11]*When he reached a certain place, he stopped for the night because the sun had set. Taking one of the stones there, he put it under his head and lay down to sleep.* [12]*He had a dream in which he saw a stairway resting on the earth, with its top reaching to heaven, and the angels of God were ascending and descending on it.* [13]*There above it stood the LORD, and he said: "I am the LORD, the God of your father Abraham and the God of Isaac. I will give you and your descendants the land on which you are lying.* [14]*Your descendants will be like the dust of the earth, and you will spread out to the west and to the east, to the north and to the south. All peoples on earth will be blessed through you and your offspring.* [15]*I am with you and will watch over you wherever you go, and I will bring you back to this land. I will not leave you until I have done what I have promised you."* [16]*When Jacob awoke from his sleep, he thought, "Surely the LORD is in this place, and I was not aware of it."* [17]*He was afraid and said, "How awesome is this place! This is none other than the house of God; this is the gate of heaven."* [18]*Early the next morning Jacob took the stone he had placed under his head and set it up as a pillar and poured oil on top of it.* [19]*He called that place Bethel (which means house of God).*

*John 1:14*

[14]*The Word became flesh and made his dwelling (tabernacle) among us. We have seen his glory, the glory of the One and Only, who came from the Father, full of grace and truth.*

*John 1:43-51*

[43]*The next day Jesus decided to leave for Galilee. Finding Philip, he said to him, "Follow me."* [44]*Philip, like Andrew*

*and Peter, was from the town of Bethsaida.* <sup>45</sup>*Philip found Nathanael and told him, "We have found the one Moses wrote about in the Law, and about whom the prophets also wrote—Jesus of Nazareth, the son of Joseph."* <sup>46</sup>*"Nazareth! Can anything good come from there?" Nathanael asked. "Come and see," said Philip.* <sup>47</sup>*When Jesus saw Nathanael approaching, he said of him, "Here is a true Israelite, in whom there is nothing false."* <sup>48</sup>*"How do you know me?" Nathanael asked. Jesus answered, "I saw you while you were still under the fig-tree before Philip called you."* <sup>49</sup>*Then Nathanael declared, "Rabbi, you are the Son of God; you are the King of Israel."* <sup>50</sup>*Jesus said, "You believe because I told you I saw you under the fig-tree. You shall see greater things than that."* <sup>51</sup>*He then added, "I tell you the truth, you shall see heaven open, and the angels of God ascending and descending on the Son of Man."*

*John 4:21-23*

<sup>21</sup>*Jesus declared, "Believe me, woman, a time is coming when you will worship the Father neither on this mountain nor in Jerusalem.* <sup>22</sup>*You Samaritans worship what you do not know; we worship what we do know, for salvation is from the Jews.* <sup>23</sup>*Yet a time is coming and has now come when the true worshippers will worship the Father in spirit and truth."*

Walking into Durham Cathedral has always been a wonderful experience for me. Here is a cathedral of majesty, of awe, yet also solid and earthy. Some cathedrals, like York Minster, are light and airy, soaring to the heavens. But Durham is strong and immovable, a testimony to God the rock. It is built on a peninsula of the River Wear, on an incised meander for the geographically-minded, so that it rises above and dominates the surrounding countryside. It also sends spiritual shivers down the spine when one realises the spiritual heritage: the early Celtic saints evangelising the area; the bones of St. Cuthbert; the medieval church maintaining the faith; the reformation in the north of England; the great scholastic bishops connected with the university; and the church of an ancient market town and mining area. This is just a little bit about Durham Cathedral, a great church in a land of great churches. Imagine for a moment someone said, "I am going to embody all that that church means, so that it will now be made redundant. Indeed, it will be destroyed while I will become the focus." You would think that they were mad. Yet this is exactly what Jesus did.

I said earlier that one of the most remarkable things about studying the temple is that it brings in all the great doctrines of the church, but in (for me at least) a new way. Some might have taken that with a pinch of salt; the more theologically minded might be saying by now, "what about the incarnation?" Well, here it is. Actually, it is not so surprising, because God promised to dwell with his people in the tabernacle and temple, even if he was unapproachable. Now God becomes approachable, and John tells us, "he tabernacled among us". It is usually translated as "dwelt among us", but actually the verb is to tabernacle. It is more than just a casual reference to Jesus pitching his tent around us. For those with ears to hear, the temple/tabernacle itself has come to be with us. So it is not so far-fetched to us the example of Durham Cathedral. Actually, it does not go far enough, for great as Durham might be, it cannot compare with the temple in Jerusalem in Jesus' day.

John 1 is John's own way of telling the nativity story. His emphasis is on the word becoming flesh, but he also includes the tabernacle becoming flesh. Both are absurd ideas. It is as incomprehensible as Jesus telling Nicodemus he needed to be born again. How can language become flesh and blood? How can a building become flesh and blood? In reality what this means is that everything the tabernacle was is summed up in Jesus. He is a living, walking, breathing temple for those who met him. For those who know him today, he is still.

A little further on in the first chapter of John's gospel is the story of Nathanael. Philip finds Nathanael of Cana and tells him that he has found the one Moses and the prophets wrote about, namely Jesus of Nazareth, son of Joseph. (To this day in the Middle East people will be introduced as from such and such a place, and son of so and so). Nathanael, perhaps because he was from a neighbouring village to Nazareth, asks if anything good can come from there. There is always local rivalry between villages; this is an example. Nathanael is a straight-speaking, bluff kind of guy. He doesn't mince his words. Philip can only say to him, "Come and see". Often we waste words in witness when we argue. Philip has no argument except the obvious: find out for yourself! Yet it is Jesus who sees Nathanael approaching, and it is Jesus who begins the conversation. The N.I.V. at this point is not a literal translation. William Temple gives a fascinating rendition: "Behold, truly an Israelite in whom there is no Jacob!"[1] It is not that Nathanael is a true Israelite (there were many of those) but that he had no deception in him. The word used is that used for Jacob, the deceiver, who became Israel. Jesus knows his heart, and welcomes him as one like the transformed Jacob.

Nathanael is amazed, and wants to know how Jesus knew him. Jesus says he saw him under the fig tree, even before Philip had called him. What was Nathanael doing under the fig tree? Perhaps he was wrestling in prayer, as Jacob had done of old. Perhaps, whatever his posture, Jesus saw straight into his heart and knew that he was not a like Jacob. In any case, Nathanael does not only feel complemented, he feels he has had his inner being revealed, and he immediately makes a magnificent confession. "Rabbi, you are the Son of God; you are the King of Israel". Nathanael recognises Jesus as his religious teacher, as one who is godly ("son of" is a way of expressing character) and as the King of Israel. One leads to the next, the highest title being King. In reality Jesus was the one and only Son of God, but Nathanael didn't understand that at this time. Yet, Jesus tells him, I haven't really done anything that wonderful yet. In the climax to the incident, he says, "I tell you the truth, you will see heaven open, and the angels of God ascending and descending on the Son of Man."

The "you" here is plural; Jesus is speaking to the whole group. But we are back with Jacob and the incident of the ladder to heaven with angels going up and down. As the angels went up and down

---

[1] William Temple, *Readings in St. John's Gospel* [first and second series], St Martin's Library 1961 p.29

to and from Jacob, so they will on Jesus. As Jacob saw heaven opened, so will Jesus. And as Jacob is Israel in the making, so now is Jesus. He is the new Israel. And as Jacob's descendants were promised the land on which he lay, so Jesus will conquer all as part of the Kingdom of God. Those disciples will see all this. And even more than that, since Jacob named the place Bethel, the house of God, we also have a new place for the house of God. For Jacob the place of God, Bethel, was located at the end of the ladder. Now the ladder reaches down to Jesus, the new Israel, the Messiah. The temple and Israel is among them: here there is no deceit, and it is meant for followers like Nathanael, who are also not deceitful. Jesus reinforces the strength of this by giving himself the title "Son of Man", the title given to the one in Daniel 7 who ascends in clouds of glory to the Ancient of Days. Heaven is opened because the Son of Man is with us.

How did they experience this vision? Indeed, how do we see this vision? The disciples saw the reality of the cross, the resurrection and the ascension. They saw miracles, heard teaching and experienced the Holy Spirit come to them. They saw heaven open, and communication open between Jesus and God. Today we may not see this physically with our eyes, but we can experience it in our hearts in a remarkably similar way. In John 4 Jesus speaks of the worship of God being neither on Mount. Gerizim (the Samaritan mountain), nor on Mount. Zion, but the worship will be in spirit and truth. The temple has become the embodiment of spirit and truth: it is Jesus, who is the place of sacrifice as well as the sacrifice itself. Today, as we know Jesus among us, we can worship in spirit and truth because he is the truth and the Holy Spirit is his true spirit with us. The temple, the place of worship, is among us.

Christ is our temple. He came to earth as a baby to become the temple. Nothing is more absurd and marvellous.

### Questions to consider

In what ways is Jesus "tabernacling" among us now?
What difference does it make if Jesus is both Israel and temple?
How can we worship "in the spirit" today?

# 20. The Raising of the Temple

*Ezekiel 37:24-28*

24 " *'My servant David will be king over them, and they will all have one shepherd. They will follow my laws and be careful to keep my decrees.* 25*They will live in the land I gave to my servant Jacob, the land where your fathers lived. They and their children and their children's children will live there for ever, and David my servant will be their prince for ever.* 26*I will make a covenant of peace with them; it will be an everlasting covenant. I will establish them and increase their numbers, and I will put my sanctuary among them for ever.* 27*My dwelling-place will be with them; I will be their God, and they will be my people.* 28*Then the nations will know that I the* LORD *make Israel holy, when my sanctuary is among them for ever.' "*

*John 2:18-22*

18*Then the Jews demanded of him, "What miraculous sign can you show us to prove your authority to do all this?"* 19*Jesus answered them, "Destroy this temple, and I will raise it again in three days."* 20*The Jews replied, "It has taken forty–six years to build this temple, and you are going to raise it in three days?"* 21*But the temple he had spoken of was his body.* 22*After he was raised from the dead, his disciples recalled what he had said. Then they believed the Scripture and the words that Jesus had spoken.*

*Acts 7:48-56*

48*"However, the Most High does not live in houses made by men. As the prophet says:* 49 " *'Heaven is my throne, and the earth is my footstool. What kind of house will you build for me? says the Lord. Or where will my resting place be?* 50*Has not my hand made all these things?'* 51*"You stiff–necked people, with uncircumcised hearts and ears! You are just like* *your fathers: You always resist the Holy Spirit! 52Was there ever a prophet your fathers did not persecute? They even killed those who predicted the coming of the Righteous One. And now you have betrayed and murdered him— 53you who have received the law that was put into effect through angels but have not obeyed it." 54When they heard this, they were furious and gnashed their teeth at him. 55But Stephen, full of the Holy Spirit, looked up to heaven and saw the glory of God, and Jesus standing at the right hand of God. 56"Look," he said, "I see heaven open and the Son of Man standing at the right hand of God."*

On August 21, 1969 an Australian called Michael Rohan went to Jerusalem and visited the temple Mount, the place where the temple used to stand. He went to the Al-Aqsa mosque and tried to set fire to it. He failed and was arrested. When questioned, he gave his reasons for his actions. He claimed that he was "the Lord's emissary" acting upon divine instructions in accordance with the Book of Zechariah. He claimed that he had tried to destroy the Al-Aqsa Mosque in order to enable the Jews of Israel to rebuild the temple on the Temple Mount and thus hasten the second coming of Jesus as the Messiah to rule the world for one thousand years. Rohan was a member of the Worldwide Church of God, a heretical sect that had a number of strange beliefs, although he was widely reported simply as a Christian at the time. In any case his understanding of Zechariah (or our reading from Ezekiel 37) is held by many Bible-believing Christians to mean that the temple will be rebuilt.

This chapter is all about the raising up of the temple. In ordinary English or Greek, "to raise up" can be used regarding a building, as well as a dead person or simply getting out of bed! It is an ambiguous phrase: "he is risen" can apply to resurrection or a tardy teenager emerging in the late morning. We might easily say, "It's rising up" to a tower block under construction. When Jesus said, "Destroy this temple, and I will raise it again in three days", his

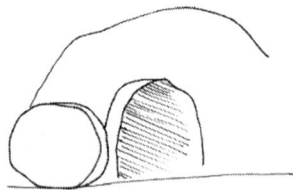

words had only one obvious meaning. He would physically rebuild the temple in three days. It was inconceivable, of course, but the sense was perfectly understandable to his listeners. It crossed no-one's mind that he was speaking of a bodily resurrection from the dead, let alone his own.

When Jesus visited the Temple Mount, there was actually a temple in existence. Michael Rohan faced a different situation. He saw two mosques where he believed there should be a great temple for God. He wanted to see Jesus return and believed, foolishly, that to help the Jews rebuild the temple would hasten that day. From his perspective and from ours today, it is understandable. The predictions in books like Ezekiel and Zechariah are quite clear. The temple must be rebuilt before the Messiah can reign. (Our reading from Ezekiel also speaks of the return of the Jews to the land and their rule under one king for ever. Briefly, this was partially fulfilled before the time of Jesus, and a complete fulfilment began in his work on the cross.) The theory is that since the temple is not rebuilt, the end cannot come until it is. But in Jesus' time they had a truly splendid temple, and they were keeping the outward form of the law pretty well. The people were back in the land. Only one part of the prophetic jigsaw was missing: they needed a king, another David. And the people hoped (and the Pharisees feared) that it would be Jesus.

This is where the story gets extraordinary. Jesus was not the prophet or king they expected. He did not make the temple perfect. Rather he predicted its destruction. He did not claim a throne by force, like King David. He went to his throne like a lamb to the slaughter. It is a retrograde step, it is something profoundly anti-Jesus, to expect the temple to be rebuilt as a fulfilment of prophecy. The temple may be rebuilt on day, I do not know. But this I know, if it is rebuilt it will not be a fulfilment of prophecy. It will not be in line with God's will. Why? Because the temple is rebuilt, raised, already, and it will stand for eternity. "I will put my sanctuary among them forever" has happened, and cannot happen again. "My dwelling place will be with them" is the wonderful reality for all those who know Jesus.

Look at Stephen's speech in Acts. "The most high does not live in houses made by men," he says, quoting scripture. "You have betrayed and murdered the Righteous One…look, I see heaven open and the Son of Man standing at the right hand of God." It is this linkage between the Messiah risen with God and God not living in a man-made temple that throws his accusers into a fury and causes them to stone Stephen to death. He is saying what Jesus taught, that the dwelling place of God is located in the Christ. Moreover heaven is open and God is now dwelling with us.

It is at this point that we should get excited as Christians. Jesus is risen, Jesus is alive. Of course there is no longer any need for a temple on Temple Mount in Jerusalem. In 1009 the Muslim Caliph Hakim ordered the destruction of the Church of the Holy Sepulchre, including the cave where Jesus was buried. This destruction was a dreadful sacrilege but it does not affect the Christian faith at all. We do not need the place of Jesus' burial to worship any more than we need the temple. We have Jesus himself, and he is the temple. One cannot blame those who heard him speak of raising up the temple in three days for not understanding. Even John says, "After he was raised from the dead, his disciples recalled what he had said". It was not easy to get it first time around! But now, for us, it is. The temple was the dwelling place of God, but God came to earth and dwelt among us. More, he rose from the dead, and lives with us eternally. The temple was the place of sacrifice, so we could come to God, but Jesus himself is the sacrifice for eternity. What has happened is that the impermanent, the things that could not exist for eternity, have been replaced by the eternal.

It is because of this that we can live in Christ. The writer to the Hebrews deals with this at length when he speaks about the tabernacle. "Their sins and lawless acts I will remember no more. And where these have been forgiven, there is no longer any sacrifice for sin. Therefore we have confidence to enter the Most Holy Place by the blood of Jesus…let us draw near to God." (Hebrews 10:17-22). God is among us and we can come to him. I suppose in a way it is putting the same thing in a different way. The circle of the realm of God had intersected with the circle of his world through Jesus; the intersection is what Jesus called the Kingdom of God, and those who follow Jesus are in it.

The writer to the Hebrews finishes his section with a verse that should convince once and for all the folly of trying to rebuild the temple, "For in just a very little while he who is coming will come and will not delay". (Hebrews 10:37) This is God's timetable, not man's.

We need to put this into practice. God is calling us to live now as those who are worshipping in the eternal temple. How do we put the resurrection into practice in the world? It is to take part in resurrection by building the new resurrection temple, the body of Christ. For the astonishing thing is that he considers his church to be his body and the temple. In other words, the resurrection that happened in his flesh is extended to his people. It can continue in us. In fact, if his resurrection is to bear fruit, it must continue in us.

**Questions to consider**

Can the church ever be as perfect as the resurrected Jesus?

How can our church become more like resurrection people?

What can we do to make it more like his perfect resurrection?

# 21. The Living Stone

*Psalm 118:19-27*

<sup>19</sup>*Open for me the gates of righteousness; I will enter and give thanks to the LORD.* <sup>20</sup>*This is the gate of the LORD through which the righteous may enter.* <sup>21</sup>*I will give you thanks, for you answered me; you have become my salvation.* <sup>22</sup>*The stone the builders rejected has become the capstone;* <sup>23</sup>*the LORD has done this, and it is marvellous in our eyes.* <sup>24</sup>*This is the day the LORD has made; let us rejoice and be glad in it.* <sup>25</sup>*O LORD, save us; O LORD, grant us success.* <sup>26</sup>*Blessed is he who comes in the name of the LORD. From the house of the LORD we bless you.* <sup>27</sup>*The LORD is God, and he has made his light shine upon us. With boughs in hand, join in the festal procession up to the horns of the altar.*

*Mark 12:1-12*

<sup>1</sup>*He then began to speak to them in parables: "A man planted a vineyard. He put a wall around it, dug a pit for the winepress and built a watchtower. Then he rented the vineyard to some farmers and went away on a journey.* <sup>2</sup>*At harvest time he sent a servant to the tenants to collect from them some of the fruit of the vineyard.* <sup>3</sup>*But they seized him, beat him and sent him away empty–handed.* <sup>4</sup>*Then he sent another servant to them; they struck this man on the head and treated him shamefully.* <sup>5</sup>*He sent still another, and that one they killed. He sent many others; some of them they beat, others they killed.* <sup>6</sup>*He had one left to send, a son, whom he loved. He sent him last of all, saying, 'They will respect my son.'* <sup>7</sup>*But the tenants said to one another, 'This is the heir. Come, let's kill him, and the inheritance will be ours.'* <sup>8</sup>*So they took him and killed him, and threw him out of the vineyard.* <sup>9</sup>*What then will the owner of the vineyard do? He will come and kill those tenants and give the vineyard to others.* <sup>10</sup>*Haven't you read this scripture: 'The stone the builders rejected has become the capstone;*

> [11]*the Lord has done this, and it is marvellous in our eyes'?"*
> [12]*Then they looked for a way to arrest him because they knew he had spoken the parable against them. But they were afraid of the crowd; so they left him and went away.*

*1 Peter 2:4-10*

> [4]*As you come to him, the living Stone—rejected by men but chosen by God and precious to him—* [5]*you also, like living stones, are being built into a spiritual house to be a holy priesthood, offering spiritual sacrifices acceptable to God through Jesus Christ.* [6]*For in Scripture it says: "See, I lay a stone in Zion, a chosen and precious cornerstone, and the one who trusts in him will never be put to shame."*
> [7]*Now to you who believe, this stone is precious. But to those who do not believe, "The stone the builders rejected has become the capstone,"* [8]*and, "A stone that causes men to stumble and a rock that makes them fall." They stumble because they disobey the message—which is also what they were destined for.* [9]*But you are a chosen people, a royal priesthood, a holy nation, a people belonging to God, that you may declare the praises of him who called you out of darkness into his wonderful light.* [10]*Once you were not a people, but now you are the people of God; once you had not received mercy, but now you have received mercy.*

The way from the city of David to the temple was, and still is, steep and difficult. The city, unusually, is built on quite a slope. If you are fit, it is not a long walk, about ten minutes. The Jerusalem of King Solomon was not large by our standards. If you go there today, it looks just like a poor area, apart from the archeological remains. But today the houses are separated from the Temple Mount by a road and the medieval wall. That would not have been the case when Psalm 118 was written. It is one of the hallel psalms, psalms of praise written when the worshippers went up to worship God at the temple. They processed straight from the city to the temple with branches waved in celebration (v.27). They went in through the gate of the Lord (v.20) as the righteous, that is to say,

those who were vindicated by
him. The Lord had saved them.
In the psalm they then sang,
"The stone the builders rejected
has become the capstone" (v.22)
This was a strange thing to say!
Were they saluting a real stone
that the builders had rejected
which unexpectedly fitted in well as the keystone of the temple? Or
perhaps there had just been a battle in which an unregarded warrior
had played the key part in winning. Most likely it reminded them
that, as a people, they were nothing special but were chosen by God
for a vital ministry. This enigmatic little verse is one of the most
quoted verses in the New Testament.

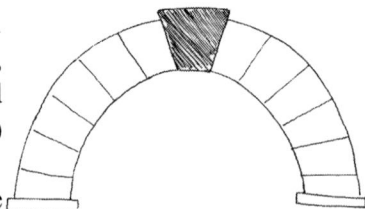

Many hundreds of years later the prophet Jesus entered
Jerusalem as a king, and the people sung psalms, including Psalm
118, and waved palm branches. He came in by a different gate,
the eastern one from the Mount of Olives rather than the southern
from the city of David, but it was a similar kind of occasion. This
began a week of teaching in the temple courts by Jesus, and he
told the parable of the Tenants (Mark 12). He told the story of the
vineyard where the absentee landlord tried to claim his share of
the crop, but his messengers were rejected, being stoned, beaten or
killed. Finally, when he sends his son, the tenants kill him as well
because they want to take over the vineyard. Jesus then gives them
the terrible news: they are the ones who rejected the capstone! They
threw aside the most important of all.

The parable needs a little more unpacking. It is an allegory; that is
to say, elements in the story represent something else. The vineyard
in the Old Testament is Israel, God's people. The tenants, who have
been given temporary care over it, are the leaders of the time (as
they rightly understood, v.12). The messengers are the prophets,
presumably up to John the Baptist, and the son is Jesus himself.
The tenants, Jesus is saying, are trying to usurp God himself. This
is what Jesus is saying to them, in the temple itself.

When he quotes Psalm 118 there is a play on words; the word
for son in Aramaic is *ben*; the word for stone *eben*. He knows that

he is being rejected, and that his rejection is not yet complete. That will come with death in a few days. They will kill him as well, but he will become the capstone of the temple.

This quote is then picked up elsewhere. In Acts 4:11, Peter uses it when he addresses the Sanhedrin itself, and tells them that salvation is found in no-one else. Paul quotes it in Ephesians 2:20, in a passage about the church. And Peter uses it up again in 1 Peter 2:7. Peter builds on the imagery to add two more functions for the stone. First he says it is a stumbling stone. It is "a stone that causes men to stumble and a rock that makes them fall." This is a quote from Isaiah 8:14, but it could equally be from the vision of Daniel 2 where the rock destroyed the pagan nations represented by the statue of Nebuchadnezzar's dream. Jesus then is the stone over which many stumble, in particular a stumbling block to the Jews. This rock is an offense, because it has been rejected. The curse of the cross runs deep with many still today. Jews and Muslims alike look to the temple mount as the place to worship God, but stumble over the part of the building rejected. Jesus is an offense because he was humiliated and suffered. The power of God was not seen in him. If he was God's son, God would have saved him. If he was God's son, he would not have been condemned as a criminal, or crucified in the first place. Sometimes we fail to realise the dynamic uniqueness of our faith. Often we fail to live up to it. The one we worship was crucified, and that is the glory.

Yet at the same time Peter calls Jesus the *living* stone. "Come to him, the living stone—rejected by men but chosen by God and precious to him (v.4). How can a stone live? It is an absurd idea. But Jesus is the capstone and the stumbling stone. He is also alive. If Jesus died, he also rose again. He is alive, and so we must come to him. Something new has happened in Christ that is unique.

When you go to Jerusalem today you see the Temple Mount as the focus of two religions. On the western side, is the famous western wall, where the Jews go to pray, the men on one side, the women on the other. The stones are huge, all that is left of the Herodian temple of Jesus' time. There are acts of great piety going on, and you see prayers written on paper put into the cracks of the wall. Above, on the mount itself, there are two mosques, and equal acts of piety. There is a large *maghssal*, so that worshippers can wash before entering. Inside there is the familiar form of Muslim worship. One can't help but be impressed by such sincere worship but the stones are dead. We all know Christians who have taken buildings too seriously, but the truth is that the stones are of limited importance for us. We have a living stone.

Here we come full circle. The living stone is also the capstone of the new temple. Peter says that "you also, like living stones, are being built into a spiritual house". The life of the risen Christ is imparted into his followers, who are joined with him to become a spiritual house. We need to investigate this in much more detail, but the essential point is made. The temple is rebuilt, not only in the body of the incarnate Christ, but also in the fellowship his followers have in him. We too have our acts of piety, but they do not need a place, rather they need a company of fellow believers rooted in the living Christ. The temple is rebuilt in us.

When pilgrims go to the land where Jesus walked, the churches there now say, do not go only to the dead stones, but visit the living stones as well. I have talked to pilgrim parties who have been exhausted by the relentless pursuit of holy sites, but who have not had fellowship with a local Christian in their whole time. It is a good lesson. We can learn much from visiting sites, but we can always learn more from the living stones who have fellowship with the Living Stone. So as we move on to consider how we are the temple of living stones, we need to know if the Living Stone is in our midst. If a believer from, say, Jerusalem, would he recognise Jesus amongst us, or shake his head sadly and say, these are dead stones. Do we reject the capstone, the living stone, or do we joyfully make him our focus, our head, our origin?

### Questions to consider

Think of all the times in the Gospels that a stone or a rock is used as imagery. Then see how this can relate to Jesus and/or the temple.

Meditate on those passages, seeing Jesus himself as the living rock.

# 22. The Living Stones

*1 Peter 2:4-10*

*⁴As you come to him, the living Stone—rejected by men but chosen by God and precious to him— ⁵you also, like living stones, are being built into a spiritual house to be a holy priesthood, offering spiritual sacrifices acceptable to God through Jesus Christ. ⁶For in Scripture it says: "See, I lay a stone in Zion, a chosen and precious cornerstone, and the one who trusts in him will never be put to shame."*

*⁷Now to you who believe, this stone is precious. But to those who do not believe, "The stone the builders rejected has become the capstone," ⁸and, "A stone that causes men to stumble and a rock that makes them fall." They stumble because they disobey the message—which is also what they were destined for. ⁹But you are a chosen people, a royal priesthood, a holy nation, a people belonging to God, that you may declare the praises of him who called you out of darkness into his wonderful light. ¹⁰Once you were not a people, but now you are the people of God; once you had not received mercy, but now you have received mercy.*

*Matthew 16:16-19*

*¹⁶Simon Peter answered, "You are the Christ, the Son of the living God." ¹⁷Jesus replied, "Blessed are you, Simon son of Jonah, for this was not revealed to you by man, but by my Father in heaven. ¹⁸And I tell you that you are Peter, and on this rock I will build my church, and the gates of Hades will not overcome it. ¹⁹I will give you the keys of the kingdom of heaven."*

In many countries in the world there are expatriate churches. Not just western expatriates, but people from many different countries. Often they exist because they all speak a language that is different from their host country. The most common language for this is English, because many have English as their second or even third language. My church in Beirut was like this. There was one congregation for Arabic-speakers, another for English-speakers. The latter may have been able to speak English, but the English were in a definite minority. There were people from the U.S., Canada, New Zealand, Australia, the U.K., Holland, Sweden and more from western countries. But people also came from Sudan, Ethiopia, Sri Lanka, the Philippines, Kenya, South Africa (black and white), Indonesia and Arab countries including Jordan, Syria, Egypt and, of course, Lebanon. On an average Sunday there would be thirty nationalities from about a hundred adults. And although the church was Anglican, these folk represented over twenty denominations: Maronite, Baptist, Orthodox of different types, Pentecostal, Mennonite, Brethren, Roman Catholic, Baptist, Presbyterian and even Anglican. How was it possible to keep all this together? There were various reasons: giving Holy Communion prominence together with biblical-preaching was one; the lack of other churches was another. However as time went on, an understanding grew that we were the body of Christ in a way that went beyond what we found in our own national churches. Our diversity made us a little more like the heavenly temple that we already make up. "You, like living stones, are being built into a spiritual house, offering spiritual sacrifices acceptable to God through Jesus Christ". Our basis was a unity based in Christ that went beyond denomination and nationality.

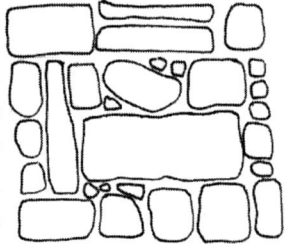

Jesus is the foundation stone of the church, but those who are part of him are described as living stones. We are those who make the living temple. We need to go back to the time of the early church to realise what an astonishing claim this was. In any city in the Roman world, at the centre of the town, there would be a great temple. Walk through the ruins of any town from Roman times and the most prominent feature remaining is likely to be a temple. For example, in the Greco-Roman town of Jerash in modern Jordan, there are still remains of baths, a hippodrome, two theatres, a triumphal arch and a beautiful colonnaded street; but high above them all are the remaining columns of the temple of Artemis. A rival, equally high, was the temple of Zeus. Contemporaries of Peter, whether Jew or Gentile, all expected that a temple would be the focus of the religion, no matter which religion it was. Religion was not possible without a temple. The temple was the place of the priests, the place of the sacrifices and the focus of sacred days. In modern society there are also gods and temples when people put something above all else and effectively worship. In our great cities there are places that can become temples by the devotion of their adherents: a stock exchange (for the god mammon/money), stadia (for the modern god of sport) and whole streets of neon (for the god Aphrodite/sex). Here, today, there are the equivalent of priests and sacrifices. To take one example, a stockbroker may be compared to a priest. He is an expert in his field, acting as an intermediary between his god (money or stocks) and the people, his clients. His sacrifice for his bonus and prestige may be everything otherwise worthwhile: time, health, marriage and children. And his god may (and often does) betray him. The cult of the temple is both ancient and modern. (Of course, let me add rapidly, a stockbroker can also be an honest Christian who puts Christ first! It all depends on what is worshipped and what is simply an occupation.)

Peter, with all the early Christian writers, breaks the mould. There was no need for a physical temple because for Christians the temple exists in the people of faith. The focus shifts to the people themselves. Imagine what this means for a moment. No longer is there a sacred action that must happen in a certain place. It can happen anywhere. No longer is there a professional priesthood whom the people service. The people themselves are the priesthood. No longer is there a need to challenge in the market-place of religions, demanding your spot of sacred soil. The holy is with you, wherever you are.

All this is saying in other words what we know instinctively as Christians. Where two or three Christians are gathered, Jesus is there. It is not, notice, when two or three are gathered in church. We know full well that Holy Communion and baptism, the two rites commanded by Jesus, can happen anywhere. Less universally acceptable is the priesthood of all believers. The calling out of certain believers to lead worship can be justified by the need for special training. However some churches (especially non-Protestants) believe in a professional priesthood as necessary mediators between humankind and God. Nevertheless Peter affirms that together the people of God make up true priesthood. There is no longer any necessity for a mediator. Together we can all now offer spiritual sacrifices acceptable to God. How is this possible? Simply because Jesus made the overarching sacrifice on the cross. The great mediation and sacrifice has happened, and now we all have the right to offer praise to God.

Some critics of religion have suggested that praise of God is not uplifting, rather that it is demeaning. That is to misunderstand the greatness of God and our position before him. To offer praise to one who is greater is not something demeaning or inhuman. Rather it is enjoyable and thrilling. Imagine for a moment we are in the presence of a great sportsman who has just done some marvellous deed. Recently the England cricket team won the Ashes. All the cricket commentators were falling over themselves to praise Andrew "Freddie" Flintoff. Everyone wanted to meet him: the prime minister, the Lord Mayor of London, thousands of fans. Everyone wanted to be in his presence, to soak up the reflected glory. This is only a small picture of what it is be like to be with Almighty God. But what if you have never heard of Freddie Flintoff? What if cricket means less than nothing to you? Then you would not notice Freddie Flintoff if he walked past you in the street. This is the position of the non-believer in not appreciating the greatness of God. Why praise God unless we have witnessed his greatness?

The living stones of the temple above all should be those who understand the greatness of God. If we are the new temple, with Jesus as our keystone, then God is in our midst. The whole point of the temple is that is where God promised to be. If we are those who trust in the work of Jesus for our salvation, then God is in us because we are the living stones of the temple. We have been called out of darkness into light; once we were not his people, now we are. We belong to him. He is in us as he promised.

There is a final point. The living stones of the temple, built on the rock of Christ, can only exist together. There is a sense in which God exists in every single Christian. It is even truer that he exists as we are bound together as his temple, the local church in different places and the church universal. If we want to know God in our midst, we must be bound together. This is a great challenge to us, the maintenance of the kingdom of heaven by being church. The church today is greatly distrusted, to some extent with good reason. All institutions are out of fashion in the west, and the church is certainly an institution. For many the church, local, national and international is irredeemably marred by sexual abuse, sexism, self-centredness, hypocrisy and in-fighting. Yet for us, if we are part of the true church, we know something else. Despite the difficulties, our presence together leads to the Holy Spirit of God in our midst. Astonishingly, as we realise that our true selves are not wretched sinful human beings but living stones of God's temple, we start to know him better and better. The blessing of God is that we can be living stones together as God temple, filled and sustained by his glory.

## Questions to consider

What are the temples of the modern world?

How can we best be church today?

There are no denominations in God's presence. How easy will it be for you to give up some precious beliefs when you face God?

What language will we speak in heaven?

# 23. The Twelve Pillars of the Temple

*Exodus 24:1-12*

¹*Then he said to Moses, "Come up to the LORD, you and Aaron, Nadab and Abihu, and seventy of the elders of Israel. You are to worship at a distance,* ²*but Moses alone is to approach the LORD; the others must not come near. And the people may not come up with him."* ³*When Moses went and told the people all the LORD's words and laws, they responded with one voice, "Everything the LORD has said we will do."* ⁴*Moses then wrote down everything the LORD had said. He got up early the next morning and built an altar at the foot of the mountain and set up twelve stone pillars representing the twelve tribes of Israel.* ⁵*Then he sent young Israelite men, and they offered burnt offerings and sacrificed young bulls as fellowship offerings to the LORD.* ⁶*Moses took half of the blood and put it in bowls, and the other half he sprinkled on the altar.* ⁷*Then he took the Book of the Covenant and read it to the people. They responded, "We will do everything the LORD has said; we will obey."* ⁸*Moses then took the blood, sprinkled it on the people and said, "This is the blood of the covenant that the LORD has made with you in accordance with all these words."* ⁹*Moses and Aaron, Nadab and Abihu, and the seventy elders of Israel went up* ¹⁰*and saw the God of Israel. Under his feet was something like a pavement made of sapphire, clear as the sky itself.* ¹¹*But God did not raise his hand against these leaders of the Israelites; they saw God, and they ate and drank.* ¹²*The LORD said to Moses, "Come up to me on the mountain and stay here, and I will give you the tablets of stone, with the law and commands I have written for their instruction."*

*Luke 6:12-16*

¹²*One of those days Jesus went out to a mountainside to pray, and spent the night praying to God.* ¹³*When morning*

*came, he called his disciples to him and chose twelve of them, whom he also designated apostles:* [14]*Simon (whom he named Peter), his brother Andrew, James, John, Philip, Bartholomew,* [15]*Matthew, Thomas, James son of Alphaeus, Simon who was called the Zealot,* [16]*Judas son of James, and Judas Iscariot, who became a traitor.*

*Matthew 19:27-28*
[27]*Peter answered him, "We have left everything to follow you! What then will there be for us?"* [28]*Jesus said to them, "I tell you the truth, at the renewal of all things, when the Son of Man sits on his glorious throne, you who have followed me will also sit on twelve thrones, judging the twelve tribes of Israel".*

Numbers matter! For the student struggling with their Maths exam, they seem never ending. Numbers fall into patterns, so that the good student can immediately see the significance: odd and even numbers; multiples of 3, or 7; prime numbers; fractions that cancel out; and so on and on, making the austere beauty of the science of Mathematics, or, alternatively, the great horror for those who are numerically challenged!

Numbers matter in the Bible as well, but in a completely different way. The student of the Bible knows full well, for example, that the numbers 7 and 40 have great symbolic importance. 7 is a number representing God (and 7 minus 1 a number representing evil), whilst 40 is a number representing a lot, or a long time. Equally, the number 12 is of great significance in the Bible.

Luke tells us very simply that Jesus called his disciples to him and chose twelve of them, whom he also designated apostles. At face value it seems an ordinary enough event, and indeed at one level it was. Jesus was choosing an inner core of disciples who would be his constant companions. These were the disciples who receive the most intimate teaching from their rabbi. This was a very reasonable method of maximising his instruction. As a rabbi, Jesus would not merely instruct, but demonstrate, show by example, every aspect of his life. Where he ate and with whom; who he commended and who he condemned; how he healed and how he kept the details of the law: all this and more were to be the daily diet of teaching for the apostles. He could not do this with a larger number.

They were also to be his friends (something of a departure from traditional rabbinical teaching, or, at the very least, an unnecessary favour) who were called to stay with him through thick and thin. They were called to follow him in what he did: healing, exorcism, preaching. This was simply an extension of traditional rabbinical teaching (what the master did, the disciples followed). What is unusual is the master, Jesus, who was doing and teaching such astonishing things.

But they were to be apostles, that is, messengers. Here we have a real indication that something very different indeed is going on. The traditional rabbis interpreted the law in a certain way and taught their disciples to do likewise. Then these disciples would be part of a certain school of interpretation within the law. Jesus wanted more than that. He wanted messengers to go and spread his message. In fact, he was the message. Demons were to be expelled in his name; the law was interpreted not by other laws but by "I say unto you"; he is the inaugurator of the Kingdom of God. These disciples were being called to be his messengers with a radical message, a message that got Jesus killed and which was to get many of them killed.

Then look at the language Luke uses. Jesus called his disciples to him and chose twelve. Calling and choosing is the prerogative of God in the Old Testament. In particular he calls and chooses Abraham and the children of Israel. Abraham is chosen and called to travel to the Promised Land. The Israelites are called out of Egypt and chosen as the people of God. Luke uses these key words to emphasise the reality of what Jesus is doing. Look afresh at what he does: he goes up a mountain to pray, and then chooses twelve. Climbing the mountain is not merely to get away from the crowds and be alone. Jesus had authority and could have asked for space if he needed it. No, praying on a mountain would have reminded every Jew there of Mount Sinai, the place of God where Moses went and Elijah went, or of Mount Zion where God commanded the temple to be built.

The passage from Exodus is the account of where Moses meets

God on the mountain. Notice what Moses does on that occasion before meeting God. He built an altar to God and set up twelve stone pillars representing the twelve tribes of Israel. And then he sacrificed on the altar, and went up the mountain to meet with God. This event is the confirmation of the covenant between the twelve tribes of Israel and almighty God. The pillars represent the tribes; the altar is the place for God. The people sacrifice to God as a sign of their acceptance of the covenant. This is the time when the chosen-ness is confirmed. Furthermore God is present in this event, a precursor of his temple/tabernacle, which is then described in great detail in the passage.

And Jesus, after his communion with God on the mountain, chooses twelve apostles. The significance of the apostles is therefore much more than just the choosing of an inner circle for teaching purposes. They are to be the new foundation of Israel, the pillars in the temple of worship, the new beginning of the people of God. Apostleship, when we speak of the original twelve, is much more than a band of messengers who will go out with the gospel. They are to be the foundation of the new Israel Jesus is creating. Jesus here is doing something similar to Moses and Elijah. He is creating a true remnant of God's people after the majority have become hopelessly corrupt. The number twelve signifies all this.

How, you might ask, did the apostles do all this? The story of the twelve goes on in the stories of the gospels and, for Peter, John and James in particular, in the stories of the Acts and in Epistles. Of the other eight original apostles, leaving out Judas Iscariot, little is heard. This does not mean that they were not extremely active; rather, it means that we have few or no reliable accounts about them.

Nevertheless, Ephesians 2:20 tells us that the people of God are built on the foundations of the apostles and the prophets. That foundation includes teaching the truth about Jesus (the writings of John, Peter and Matthew are all from the original apostles). We see the apostles filled with the Holy Spirit at Pentecost, the mark of the new remnant of Israel. We see Peter and John healing and testifying before the Sanhedrin, showing in practice evangelism, healing and acts of love. We see Peter, the leader, taking the mission to the Gentile Cornelius. This is the foundation work of the building of Gods people (remembering that Jesus is always the cornerstone).

Were they always successful? Emphatically not. Peter is proverbial for denying Jesus. James and John wanted to be Jesus' chief ministers. The disciples were incapable of performing an exorcism. There are many other examples (and no doubt many unrecorded). In all this they were human, but in God's good grace they were also our foundation.

And finally they are also the future in a startling way. Jesus says, quite straightforwardly, that they will judge the twelve tribes of Israel. This is not merely confirmation of their superiority to and replacement of the original Israel. It also shows the responsibility given to them by our Lord. He delegated his judgement to them.

The twelve apostles were more than Jesus' band of closest disciples. They are the chosen foundation of the new Israel, the vehicle for the Kingdom of God, the pillars of the new temple.

### Questions to consider

How do you think the surrounding Jews felt about Jesus openly choosing twelve?

Have you ever felt left out? How do you think those outside the twelve felt?

Look at some examples (Nicodemus is one) to see how they reacted.

Why were there no women in the twelve?

# 24. The Gentiles in the Temple

*Isaiah 42:6-7*

> [6]*"I, the LORD, have called you in righteousness; I will take hold of your hand. I will keep you and will make you to be a covenant for the people and a light for the Gentiles, [7]to open eyes that are blind, to free captives from prison and to release from the dungeon those who sit in darkness."*

*Luke 2:28-32*

> [28]*Simeon took him in his arms and praised God, saying: [29]"Sovereign Lord, as you have promised, you now dismiss your servant in peace. [30]For my eyes have seen your salvation, [31]which you have prepared in the sight of all people, [32]a light for revelation to the Gentiles and for glory to your people Israel."*

*Acts 13:46-48*

> [46]*Then Paul and Barnabas answered them boldly: "We had to speak the word of God to you first. Since you reject it and do not consider yourselves worthy of eternal life, we now turn to the Gentiles. [47]For this is what the Lord has commanded us: " 'I have made you a light for the Gentiles, that you may bring salvation to the ends of the earth.' " [48]When the Gentiles heard this, they were glad and honoured the word of the Lord; and all who were appointed for eternal life believed.*

*Ephesians 2:11-22*

> [11]*Therefore, remember that formerly you who are Gentiles by birth and called "uncircumcised" by those who call themselves "the circumcision" (that done in the body by the hands of men)—[12]remember that at that time you were separate from Christ, excluded from citizenship in Israel and foreigners to the covenants of the promise, without hope*

*and without God in the world. ¹³But now in Christ Jesus you who once were far away have been brought near through the blood of Christ. ¹⁴For he himself is our peace, who has made the two one and has destroyed the barrier, the dividing wall of hostility, ¹⁵by abolishing in his flesh the law with its commandments and regulations. His purpose was to create in himself one new man out of the two, thus making peace, ¹⁶and in this one body to reconcile both of them to God through the cross, by which he put to death their hostility. ¹⁷He came and preached peace to you who were far away and peace to those who were near. ¹⁸For through him we both have access to the Father by one Spirit. ¹⁹Consequently, you are no longer foreigners and aliens, but fellow-citizens with God's people and members of God's household, ²⁰built on the foundation of the apostles and prophets, with Christ Jesus himself as the chief cornerstone. ²¹In him the whole building is joined together and rises to become a holy temple in the Lord. ²²And in him you too are being built together to become a dwelling in which God lives by his Spirit.*

---

**Notice and warning:**
Entrance to the Temple Mount is forbidden to everyone
by Jewish Law owing to the sacredness of the place.
*The Chief Rabbinate of Israel.*

---

So reads the sign today on the entrance to the Temple Mount. Of course, not all Jewish authorities agree, and not all Jews obey. Nevertheless, it is a sign of the feelings toward the site. Run the clock back two thousand years and the restrictions were even more onerous. The temple, as we have seen, was divided into different courts, which became progressively more exclusive as you went in. The very outer court was the court of the Gentiles. It was the largest court, an extensive 35 acres in area. In this court people from all walks of life would mill about, including the moneychangers and sacrifice sellers, and, of course, non-Jews. In the centre of the Court of the Gentiles there was a balustrade surrounding all the other courts and the temple. Posted on the balustrade in Greek and

Latin was the following warning: "No foreigner is allowed within the balustrades and embankment about the sanctuary. Whoever is caught will be personally responsible for his ensuing death."

When Paul spoke of the dividing wall, the barrier, he was thinking of the law. However it was symbolised in the most powerful way by the division in the temple. The law prevented the Gentiles from entering where Jews were allowed. They were "the uncircumcised": foreigners to the promises of God. A good Jew, who kept the law, would feel polluted if a foreigner (that is, non-Jew) entered the inner courts. He would feel it a righteous act to stone such a foreigner, and hence the ancient notice.

Paul described the situation of those Gentiles in Ephesians, in one of the great New Testament passages about the temple. He said they were excluded from citizenship. That is to say, they could not be citizens of God's people, Israel. They were without hope and without God, because they were foreigners to the covenants. The words foreigner and Gentile are almost identical in the Hebrew, and the reason is that they were not part of the promises of God. The covenants were not made to them but to others. The implication here is for all the covenants, not just one, as the word is plural. The Gentiles in their court in the temple faced death if they came any nearer. They were excluded by the barrier of the law, that is to say God's promises with his people.

The impenetrability of this barrier is difficult to understand today. By calling the Jewish people God had intended that they be different and separate. The purpose was to create a holy people who kept his standards and who were obedient to him. There was a genuine separateness that had to be maintained. Yet at the same time they were supposed to be a light to the non-Jews, the Gentiles. The barrier at the time of Jesus involved a hatred and hostility that was very bitter. Through this hostility no light could shine. The separateness was never meant to lead to hatred, but rather to be attractive. When Jesus came to fulfil the prophecy in Isaiah and be the light, many Jews could not see it. When later the call to be disciples of Jesus went out, it was often the Gentiles who responded to the light rather than the Jews.

This was possible because Jesus has destroyed the barrier. This does not mean that he has destroyed the law itself. The actual relationship between what Jesus has done and the law is complicated and needs fuller treatment than is possible here. However in shorthand we can say he is the fulfilment of the law. The barrier was only temporary and through Jesus the covenant promises of God have suddenly expanded to encompass, in potential, all humanity.

Tom Wright in his commentary[1] on this passage uses an illustration which is extremely helpful. Imagine two rivers, one a small one and one a large one, which flow into one another. Downstream of the confluence you can no longer tell them apart, even though a few miles previously they were completely separate, having no contact whatsoever. If one was carrying a heavy load of silt it may even be a different colour, but nonetheless they are indistinguishable downstream because they become completely mixed. This is what God has done in Jesus with the Gentiles and the Jews. However there is one strange fact about this joining. The river takes the name of the smaller, not the greater. The name of the small river was Israel, and so is the name of the combined river. The Gentiles, as they believe in the one true God, take the identity and citizenship that God gave the Jews. They all now are covenantal people. There is complete unity where there had been division, and peace where there had been hostility.

Paul speaks of those who were near, and those who were far off, both having equal access to the Father through the Spirit of God. We can see this precisely in the structure of the temple. The Gentiles could go no further than their court or risk death. The Jews, especially the men, especially the priests, and above all the High Priest, could come closer. The High Priest could even come into the presence of God once a year in the Holy of Holies. Now it makes no difference. It does not matter how close we were to begin with or how far away we were. We all have equal access. This was achieved by Jesus on the cross. He gives us access to God

[1] N. T. Wright, *Paul for Everyone: The Prison Letters*, p.25, S.P.C.K. 2002

by his sacrifice, but an integral part of that is the sacrifice was for all, not just for Jews. The penalty of the law has been paid, and the boundaries of the covenants expanded.

Paul's conclusion is this. As fellow-citizens we are members of God's household. The foundation is the apostles and the prophets, that is, those who witnessed to the power of Christ in the early church. Jesus himself is the cornerstone, as we have already seen, but he more. Paul says that in Jesus the whole building is joined together, that he is, if you like, the cement of the bricks. The building is a holy temple, the new temple without courts dividing people up, where God himself dwells. And Paul says that those who have been saved by grace through faith (v.8) are this building. This means that there is no longer any division in humanity for those who are part of this temple. Now all can be part of the covenant, whatever their background. Paul not only includes Jews and Gentiles but also male and female and slave and free. To this list we can fairly add all races, all orientations, all disabilities, all backgrounds. The saving power of Christ and the unity that there is in him transcends every other identity. The temple is a building where everyone is united and everyone has a part. God has reunited the creatures he made in his image.

## Questions to consider

How can all the covenants be the gift for all Christians today?
Do you feel there is a group of people that you despise? Or a group of people who leave you out?
How can you help rebuild the temple by your attitude and actions?
If those who are in Christ are the people of God, how does he see the Jews today?

# 25. Building the Temple

*1 Chronicles 29:1-6*

[1]*Then King David said to the whole assembly: "My son Solomon, the one whom God has chosen, is young and inexperienced. The task is great, because this palatial structure is not for man but for the LORD God.* [2]*With all my resources I have provided for the temple of my God—gold for the gold work, silver for the silver, bronze for the bronze, iron for the iron and wood for the wood, as well as onyx for the settings, turquoise, stones of various colours, and all kinds of fine stone and marble—all of these in large quantities.* [3]*Besides, in my devotion to the temple of my God I now give my personal treasures of gold and silver for the temple of my God, over and above everything I have provided for this holy temple:* [4]*three thousand talents of gold (gold of Ophir) and seven thousand talents of refined silver, for the overlaying of the walls of the buildings,* [5]*for the gold work and the silver work, and for all the work to be done by the craftsmen. Now, who is willing to consecrate himself today to the LORD?"* [6]*Then the leaders of families, the officers of the tribes of Israel, the commanders of thousands and commanders of hundreds, and the officials in charge of the king's work gave willingly.*

*Ezra 3:1-3, 6*

[1]*When the seventh month came and the Israelites had settled in their towns, the people assembled as one man in Jerusalem.* [2]*Then Jeshua son of Jozadak and his fellow priests and Zerubbabel son of Shealtiel and his associates began to build the altar of the God of Israel to sacrifice burnt offerings on it, in accordance with what is written in the Law of Moses the man of God.* [3]*Despite their fear of the peoples around them, they built the altar on its foundation and sacrificed burnt offerings on it to the LORD, both the morning*

*and evening sacrifices. <sup>6</sup>On the first day of the seventh month they began to offer burnt offerings to the LORD, though the foundation of the LORD's temple had not yet been laid.*

*1 Corinthians 3:10-17*

<sup>10</sup>*By the grace God has given me, I laid a foundation as an expert builder, and someone else is building on it. But each one should be careful how he builds. <sup>11</sup>For no-one can lay any foundation other than the one already laid, which is Jesus Christ. <sup>12</sup>If any man builds on this foundation using gold, silver, costly stones, wood, hay or straw, <sup>13</sup>his work will be shown for what it is, because the Day will bring it to light. It will be revealed with fire, and the fire will test the quality of each man's work. <sup>14</sup>If what he has built survives, he will receive his reward. <sup>15</sup>If it is burned up, he will suffer loss; he himself will be saved, but only as one escaping through the flames. <sup>16</sup>Don't you know that you yourselves are God's temple and that God's Spirit lives in you? <sup>17</sup>If anyone destroys God's temple, God will destroy him; for God's temple is sacred, and you are that temple.*

*Matthew 7:24*

<sup>7</sup>*The wise man built his house upon the rock*

Central Beirut was terribly ravaged by the civil war. The so-called green line, the division between the two warring parties, was the land of snipers and artillery. Snipers shot from the high buildings, and the opposing artillery shot at them. The result was dreadful damage to the buildings. When the war finished, some of the buildings had to be pulled down and destroyed altogether, whilst others were renovated at great expense if they were deemed valuable enough. One building was completely torn down and a massive pit dug for the foundations, some three or four stories deep. This building was being designed to survive war and earthquake and flood! Our church in Beirut was on the green line, right next to the sea. It was built on a rocky outcrop that had survived the assault of the sea for thousands of years. Moreover it had not been structurally damaged by the war. It was built of large blocks of stone. Also it had not been high enough to be of use for snipers, and it had been surrounded by others buildings and palm trees that took the worst of the destruction. These surrounding buildings were destroyed, but the church survived and needed (compared with other places) only limited restoration.

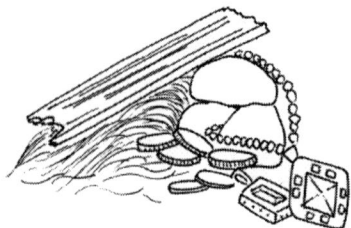

Paul uses these kinds of images to describe the church in Corinthians. He speaks of the foundation, the building materials and risk of fire. This short passage of 1 Corinthians. 3:10-17 is about how to build a church and how to ensure it survives the Day of Judgement. He also says that this building is God's temple, the place where the Holy Spirit of God resides. Paul, in his evangelistic journeys, knows that he is building the true temple of God, even while the old one still stood in Jerusalem.

First he speaks of the foundation. That foundation, he says, must be Jesus. There can be no other foundation but Jesus the Messiah. This is the only basis for any church. It is interesting that when Ezra was rebuilding the temple in Jerusalem, even before the building began, they sacrificed on the altar around which the temple would be built. In other words, the central point was the sacrificial offering. It is still true today, except that we know that that offering is our Lord Jesus on the cross. He died that we might be freed from sin and be part of his kingdom, living stones in his building. What does this mean for the evangelist and pastor today? Simply this: maintain the foundation. When we preach for conversion, we must preach Jesus. Among the faithful, the sacrifice and resurrection of Jesus is remembered in the Holy Communion, the bread and wine that he commanded us to eat in remembrance of him. The words of Jesus are remembered in the reading of the four gospels, the rest of the New Testament applies his words and actions and the Old Testament looks forward to his sacrifice. We baptise in church, again in obedience to his command, so that people can repent and symbolically come to new life in Jesus. Jesus is the foundation.

Now on this foundation the leaders can build. What are the gold, silver and precious stones that Paul speaks about? David laid aside his treasure for the building of the temple. It was the best David had, and he called on the people to do likewise. The effort of the leaders in building God's temple is to be the utmost for his glory. However that is not enough. One has to be an expert builder, like Paul. It is not enough just to give everything: that is the way to burnout and often error. For leaders, total obedience needs wisdom so that it is applied correctly. This wisdom must include the regulation of personal life and understanding of Jesus' will for the present situation. It is not enough to follow without understanding; it is not enough to understand without following. In this way expert builders are to call the church to a discipleship that is eternal. This discipleship will include giving, worship, learning, family life, preparation for death, enjoyment of life, witness to the saviour. It needs to be rounded and complete. As the members of the church move in this discipleship, based on the foundation of Christ, the temple grows.

Yet Paul then goes on to warn of the dangers of a foundation and poor building materials. He speaks of the danger of a wrong foundation. In the case of Corinth this probably meant putting too much emphasis on other people (look at the earlier verses in 1 Corinthians). Perhaps they thought that Peter should be the rock, not Jesus, following a misunderstanding of what Jesus said when he nicknamed Simon "Peter", the rock. Perhaps it was a reference to the other apostles, Peter, John and James, whom some said were the "pillars" (Galatians 2:9). This may have been the danger for Corinth, and the cult of personality still can be a danger today. Yet there are other rival "foundations" that can afflict churches: money, liturgy, social activities or the building itself. We can also relegate Jesus to being equal with other religions, or start to trust in superstitions. There are many dangers, and we must consistently come back to our Lord himself. He is the only foundation; any other will lead to destruction.

The second danger Paul mentions is building with poor materials. He talks of wood, hay and straw, materials that are highly combustible. What are these representing? In Paul's time they were probably the works of the Judaisers those who believed that Gentile Christians had to be circumcised and fulfil some aspects of the ceremonial law to be good Christians. This may seem obscure to us, but what it was doing was adding to the gospel. It is a danger for many missionaries today, not least those working amongst the Jews, if they try to accommodate their old practices. "You can't be a real Christian without having a Seder meal at Passover" could be a danger for Messianic Jews. "We have to give up alcohol to be a true Christian" is a danger for some Muslim converts. It is the "have to", the imperative, that is the danger. Yet it is not just converts from other religions who have these kinds of dangers. One long-standing church may be overly judgmental, and so fail to be merciful like Jesus. Another may be too lax, and lose the cutting edge of the need for repentance to which Christ calls us.

In fact all leaders fail to be sufficiently expert in their building and all churches will, to some extent, be made of hay and straw. This will be revealed on "the Day" as Paul call's it, the Day of Judgement. Paul's illustration here is striking. The fire on that day is not so much punishment as test. The fire is being used to test the quality of the work, and is thus judgmental. Whatever can be burned up, will be. The one who has built with good materials will receive a reward. The one who hasn't will only escape as one through fire; that is to say, like a man whose house is on fire will have to run when the fire takes hold. There is no reward, but there is loss. Note that there is no question about his salvation; the fire will not engulf him altogether. He will be saved.

Paul ends with one final note, moving on from the work of the inexpert builder to the deliberate destroyer of the local church. Here there is a question concerning ultimate salvation. Because it is God's temple, such a person must be destroyed themselves, because they are destroying what is holy. Without repentance final, destructive judgment is bound to come. That is how important God's dwelling place, his people, is to him.

**Questions to consider**

To what extent is your church based on the foundation of Jesus?

To what extent is your life based on the foundation of Jesus?

What is there in your church that is "gold and silver"?

What is there that is "straw and hay"?

How can you pray for and support your leaders in their task?

# 26. The Court of Women

*Deuteronomy 24:1-4*

> [1]*If a man marries a woman who becomes displeasing to him because he finds something indecent about her, and he writes her a certificate of divorce, gives it to her and sends her from his house,* [2]*and if after she leaves his house she becomes the wife of another man,* [3]*and her second husband dislikes her and writes her a certificate of divorce, gives it to her and sends her from his house, or if he dies,* [4]*then her first husband, who divorced her, is not allowed to marry her again after she has been defiled. That would be detestable in the eyes of the LORD. Do not bring sin upon the land the LORD your God is giving you as an inheritance.*

*Matthew 27:50, 55-61; 28:1-10*

> [50]*And when Jesus had cried out again in a loud voice, he gave up his spirit.* [55]*Many women were there, watching from a distance. They had followed Jesus from Galilee to care for his needs.* [56]*Among them were Mary Magdalene, Mary the mother of James and Joses, and the mother of Zebedee's sons.* [57]*As evening approached, there came a rich man from Arimathea, named Joseph, who had himself become a disciple of Jesus.* [58]*Going to Pilate, he asked for Jesus' body, and Pilate ordered that it be given to him.* [59]*Joseph took the body, wrapped it in a clean linen cloth,* [60]*and placed it in his own new tomb that he had cut out of the rock. He rolled a big stone in front of the entrance to the tomb and went away.* [61]*Mary Magdalene and the other Mary were sitting there opposite the tomb.* [1]*After the Sabbath, at dawn on the first day of the week, Mary Magdalene and the other Mary went to look at the tomb.* [2]*There was a violent earthquake, for an angel of the Lord came down from heaven and, going to the tomb, rolled back the stone and sat on it.* [3]*His appearance was like lightning, and his clothes were white as snow.* [4]*The*

*guards were so afraid of him that they shook and became like dead men.* ⁵*The angel said to the women, "Do not be afraid, for I know that you are looking for Jesus, who was crucified.* ⁶*He is not here; he has risen, just as he said. Come and see the place where he lay.* ⁷*Then go quickly and tell his disciples: 'He has risen from the dead and is going ahead of you into Galilee. There you will see him.' Now I have told you."* ⁸*So the women hurried away from the tomb, afraid yet filled with joy, and ran to tell his disciples.* ⁹*Suddenly Jesus met them. "Greetings," he said. They came to him, clasped his feet and worshipped him.* ¹⁰*Then Jesus said to them, "Do not be afraid. Go and tell my brothers to go to Galilee; there they will see me."*

I went into a darkened Coptic church in Old Cairo. It was the time of the midday prayers, and there were only a scattering of people, so I sat quietly near the back on the left. One or two people looked at me slightly strangely as they came in, but I assumed it was just because I was a foreigner. A few more people entered, and I started to notice a pattern. All the men were heading for the right side of the church, and the veiled women to the left: my side. I suddenly realised, to my acute discomfort, that I had sat down on the side of the women.

King Herod's temple had what was known as the court of the women. Compared with the tabernacle and Solomon's temple, the temple in Jesus' time was more complicated. The first temples had three sections: the courtyard (for the people), the Holy Place where only the priests could enter, and the Holy of Holies, where God alone dwelt. Herod's temple elaborated on this by subdividing the courtyard. This was now made up of the Court of the Gentiles, the Court of the Women, the Court of Israel and the Court of the Priests, before the Holy Place was entered. The largest of these courts was the court of the Gentiles, and the next largest the Court of the Women. Despite its name, any Jew could enter the Court of the Women. However the Court of Israel was on a raised platform above the Court of Women, and only Jewish men could go beyond the Court of Women. It provided a striking illustration that women could not enter as far as men. Not only were they prohibited from coming as close to God as men, they also could not become priests and take part in the most sacred rituals that God commanded. They were observers rather than participants.

The position of women in Jewish society in Jesus' time was very unlike our own today. The whole society was very patriarchal. Women only had significant rights in the home, although these should not be underestimated: a woman could exercise very far-reaching control from that position. From this base a woman could and did run many spheres of life. Nevertheless in general the man had great control over a woman's life. The man controlled the activities of his wife and daughters and their relationships, especially with other men. When a woman married, that control was passed from her father to her husband. Although there is evidence that a woman could sometimes be the president of a synagogue, this was not normal. In court a woman's testimony was not equal to a man, and women did not have the right to divorce. Some of these laws were from the Torah (for example, the ability of a man to divorce his wife who displeases him, whilst a woman had no such right). However many of these laws were based on the oral law, the Mishnah, which was developing in Jesus' time and would eventually be codified about 200 years later. In worship the situation was similar. A woman could and did do various things: make a Nazirite vow (Numbers 6:2) and bring sacrifices in their own right, and there were particular sacrifices relating to purification after childbirth (Leviticus 12:6, Luke 2:21-22). However the time to wait for purification varied between a boy child (seven days) and a girl child (two weeks)!

It has been suggested that God had legislated for this ordering of society (between the home and public spheres, the female and male) as he increasingly revealed himself following the fall. Jesus completes this revelation in a way that scandalised his contemporaries. He broke down the dividing wall in the temple between male and female. Jesus, as we have seen, was creating a new temple, his body, in which there was a completely different attitude to women. We cannot say that he followed a modern feminist programme (which often starts with different assumptions to

Christ). He was ordering the new temple which he was establishing in a wonderful way.

First he treats women as people full of dignity and worth, as he did men. He healed many women, including Simon's mother-in-law (Mark 1:29-31), Jairus' daughter (Mark 5:21-43) and a woman crippled eighteen years (Luke 13:11-17), whom he affirms as a daughter of Abraham. Perhaps most significant healing is the woman with a twelve year flow of blood. This woman would have been considered ritually unclean by the law (Leviticus 18), yet he allowed her to touch him, did not chastise her for doing so and then healed her. He was prepared to be considered unclean himself to allow a needy woman to be healed. As a rabbi he was not afraid to use women as a positive example of his teaching. The parable of the lost coin (Luke 15:8-10), the widow of Zarephath (Luke 4:26), the persistent widow (Luke 18) and the "widow's mite" (Matthew 12:41-44) are some examples.

Jesus also was prepared to be associated with women who were considered to be sexual sinners. This included the woman who washed his feet with her hair in the Pharisees house (Luke 7:36-50), the woman caught in adultery about to be stoned (John 8:11) and the Samaritan woman (John 4). In all these cases he faced down male disapproval (including that of his own disciples), challenged the women to change their behaviour and offered them forgiveness. He even said to the chief priests and elders in the temple that, "tax collectors and prostitutes are entering the kingdom of God ahead of you. For John came to you to show you the way of righteousness, and you did not believe him, but the tax collectors and prostitutes did." (Matthew 21:31-32) Modern secular and new age commentators seeing these sexual examples sometimes assume that he had to be motivated sexually himself. In reality this is a projection from modern western culture that is unwarranted from the biblical record.

Secondly, if Jesus presented women as people of worth, he also allowed them to be disciples. All four Gospels mention women disciples. Moreover

they were the faithful ones at his crucifixion, burial and resurrection. These women included those who were travelling with him in Galilee who had been healed by him and who were supporting him financially (Luke 8:1-3). They were also present in the Upper Room for the selection of a new apostle and to receive the Holy Spirit at Pentecost. Incidentally his own mother, Mary, was the most prominent among those female disciples.

Thirdly women acted as proclaimers of the gospel. There are Elizabeth, Mary and Anna in the stories of Jesus' birth; there is the vivid example of the Samaritan woman in John 4; above all there are the female witnesses of the resurrection. About the latter Luke says specifically that the men did not believe the women (Luke 24:11), a telling comment on who were the faithful disciples. This affirmation of women as reliable and authentic witnesses spoke eloquently against the anti-women bias at the time, when a woman's witness was deemed inferior. The new temple of God, the resurrected body of Jesus, God allowed to be announced by the witness of women.

These three areas speak strongly of Jesus attitude to women in the temple he was building. It has been said that by failing to appoint a woman to the position of one of the twelve apostles he excluded them from leadership. However, the same argument could be made about Gentiles, and we see in the early church both Gentiles and women in leadership. For example in the list of greetings to prominent church members in Rome by Paul (Romans 16) is predominantly Gentile and includes seven women. Prisca (Priscilla elsewhere) was a woman with many responsibilities; Junia is described as an outstanding apostle who was an eyewitness of the risen Jesus (see 1 Corinthians. 15:7); and Mary, Tryphena, Tryphosa and Persis are commended as hard workers in the Lord.

The question of how Jesus' attitude and teaching towards women are interpreted in the remainder of the Bible would take too long to go into here. However, in the context of the temple, a number of foundational points of interpretation should be made. In the first temple, the Garden of Eden, there is also no subservience for the woman before the fall. "God created man (i.e. humanity) in his own image, in the image of God he created him; male and female he created them" (Genesis 1:27). The image of God is equally in both sexes. In the later account of the creation of the woman the idea that she is to be a "helper" (Genesis 2:18) is not demeaning but rather, in the Hebrew, it is a term of partnership, literally "a help opposite him". In Galatians 3:27-8 Paul says that, "all of those baptised into Christ have clothed yourselves with Christ. There is neither...male or female, for you are all one in Christ Jesus." In other words, in the temple of Christ's body in the New Testament church, there is no discrimination. And at the end of the Bible in the Book of Revelation, in the final temple, there is no distinction between men and women whatsoever.

In terms of the temple, Jesus destroyed the court of the Women. He destroyed all the courts, because we now have access to the father through the son. No longer does gender divide humanity in worth or respect, for all are one in Christ.

## Questions to consider

How do you view the opposite sex? Is there any prejudice in your attitude?

Does equality in worth mean equality in role (before the final temple is here)?

Choose a gospel story where someone of the opposite sex is in a key role, and imagine you are them.

What does it feel like to be treated by Jesus in this situation?

# 27. Your Body the Temple

*Exodus 40:34-38*

> [34]*Then the cloud covered the Tent of Meeting, and the glory of the LORD filled the tabernacle.* [35]*Moses could not enter the Tent of Meeting because the cloud had settled upon it, and the glory of the LORD filled the tabernacle.* [36]*In all the travels of the Israelites, whenever the cloud lifted from above the tabernacle, they would set out;* [37]*but if the cloud did not lift, they did not set out—until the day it lifted.* [38]*So the cloud of the LORD was over the tabernacle by day, and fire was in the cloud by night, in the sight of all the house of Israel during all their travels.*

*Ezekiel 43:4-5*

> [4]*The glory of the LORD entered the temple through the gate facing east.* [5]*Then the Spirit lifted me up and brought me into the inner court, and the glory of the LORD filled the temple.*

*1 Corinthians 6:12-20*

> [12]*"Everything is permissible for me"—but not everything is beneficial. "Everything is permissible for me"—but I will not be mastered by anything.* [13]*"Food for the stomach and the stomach for food"—but God will destroy them both. The body is not meant for sexual immorality, but for the Lord, and the Lord for the body.* [14]*By his power God raised the Lord from the dead, and he will raise us also.* [15]*Do you not know that your bodies are members of Christ himself? Shall I then take the members of Christ and unite them with a prostitute? Never!* [16]*Do you not know that he who unites himself with a prostitute is one with her in body? For it is said, "The two will become one flesh."* [17]*But he who unites himself with the Lord is one with him in spirit.* [18]*Flee from sexual immorality. All other sins a man commits are outside his body, but he who sins sexually sins against his own body.* [19]*Do you not*

*know that your body is a temple of the Holy Spirit, who is in you, whom you have received from God? You are not your own;* [20]*you were bought at a price. Therefore honour God with your body.*

The painting on the ceiling of the Sistine Chapel in the Vatican is one of the most famous pieces of religious art in the world. The most reproduced part is the creation of Adam, where the figure of God reaches out to touch the naked man, with Eve, still to be created, under God's arm. However the image can also be seen another way. We are all made in the image of God, but God is still reaching out to touch us day by day. He longs to be part of us. This might be verging on blasphemy but for this verse by Paul, "Do you not know that your body is the temple of the Holy Spirit?" The idea here is that we are not merely touched by God, but that that touch leads to our filling in the same as God filled the temple in the Old Testament.

This is an outrageous, daring concept. Paul has said that the gathering of believers in a local situation is the body of Christ, the temple of God filled by his presence. Here he goes further, to say that each one of those members is individually filled with God as well. It is not only that by being in the Christian gathering that we are filled; we are also filled with God because we were individually bought back by Jesus. Paul says were bought for a price; we know that that price was Jesus death on the cross. This is a matter for awe and wonder, that God should both give himself for us and then deign to fill us with his glory when we accept his gift.

It is difficult to make too much of this. In the desert the glory of God was overwhelming. Moses could not enter the tent because the cloud of God's glory had settled there. Ezekiel saw the Lord enter his temple in all his glory, an experience linked to the activity of the Holy Spirit. And now Paul says that this same Holy Spirit has entered us because each one of us, as individuals, is a successor of the tabernacle and temple.

It is only our lack of appreciation of what the temple and the glory of God means that stops us from protesting in horror at any such thing. Sadly for many Christians the concept that we are the temple of the Holy Spirit has become a commonplace thing divorced from the original context. It becomes a vague feel good "warm fuzzy" that God is with us in some undefined way. But this is not the God of the Bible, the God of Paul and the other apostles, the God of Ezekiel and Moses. God filling us as he filled his temple may be another way of saying that we are filled with the Holy Spirit, but Paul is deliberately putting that away to bring the Corinthians (and us) up with a jolt. To be filled with God is something too wonderful for expression.

The nakedness of the man in the Sistine chapel brings home another point. God is not ashamed of his creation. The whole passage from Corinthians is about the body belonging to human beings. When Michelangelo painted in the Sistine Chapel there was a complaint that the nakedness of the human beings should be covered with fig leaves. Yet this is the very point of God's creation: there is nothing to be ashamed about the human body. It is this body, with or without clothes, that God fills with his Holy Spirit. It is this body that is compared to the temple of God. Remember the tabernacle was built precisely to God's specification. Remember Solomon's temple was built with the costliest gold and jewels. Remember Herod's temple took many decades to complete. This is how God sees his creation, the human body. Christians still have a reputation for having a Victorian, or a puritanical view of the body, and sometimes it is true. But in fact a true view of the body is God's view, namely that we are made in his image and that there is nothing bad about our bodies. We'd better believe it because our resurrection is bodily and we will live for eternity with our perfected bodies. Those bodies will be permanently filled by the Holy Spirit.

And yet, and yet, we know that our bodies are fallen and not perfect. They wear out for one thing. They sin for another. The whole reason Paul wrote in 1 Corinthians 6 as he did was because of the sin of the Corinthians. He takes the sayings of the Corinthians and answers them. "Everything is permissible for me" (v.12). Well yes, he says, but not if it becomes your God (i.e. it masters you).

Yet Paul does not reject the saying completely, rather he modifies it: "All things that my relationship with God allows are permissible". In short, he affirms the goodness of God's original creation and will.

He does something similar with a second saying, "Food for the stomach and the stomach for food" (v.13a). The Corinthians are saying that all food is good, and that the food laws no longer apply. Again Paul agrees, but orders a little bit of perspective, "God will destroy them both". In other words the natural process of the digestion system also extends to the natural disintegration of death and decay.

It is at this point that Paul disagrees with the Corinthians and takes them to task. Food and stomach, yes; body and sexual immorality, no (v.13b). It appears that the Corinthians may have been using an argument to him that ran along the following lines. God made the stomach for food and the food for the stomach, and we know that in Christ there is no restriction on what food we eat. Now God made the body with a sexual purpose, so there is no restriction on our sexual activities either. Paul answers with a resounding no, because the stomach cannot be compared with the body. The body is the temple of the Holy Spirit.

However before coming to the climax of the argument, he uses other arguments. First, the body will be resurrected in to eternity (v.14) and is not for sexual immorality. Secondly, our bodies are members of Christ's body (v.15). How then can they become united with a prostitute? Thirdly sexual intercourse brings unity of one flesh (v.16). This is a scriptural argument for the right use of sexuality, which is having one partner until death.

It seems that in Corinth there was a particular problem of sexual immorality, probably due to the number of cult prostitutes surrounding the various Greek shrines. This may be the explanation to verse 18, which appears to make sexual sin a particularly bad sin. It may be that "Every sin a man commits is outside his own body" was a slogan of those favouring free sex in Corinth, so that Paul's response is to the contrary. Sexual sin is against your own body.

This leaves open the obvious extension for our own time, namely that there are many ways of sinning against our body. Smoking, excessive alcohol, drugs, mutilation, gluttony, excessive dieting, addictive exercise and other sins are all against our body. It is true to say that we are to look after our bodies to glorify God because we are made in his image. This is not to justify a narcissistic attitude, merely to commend a sensible attitude.

For, as Paul says (v.19), "You are not your own". We now belong to Christ and are filled by the presence of the glory of God. One way to help a correct understanding of our bodies is to look into the God who is prepared to dwell within us.

## Questions to consider

How do you view your own body?

What does it mean for you "to be the temple of the Holy Spirit"?

Look at the picture of the creation of Adam by Michelangelo. What feelings does it arouse?

Can you see yourself as the man in the picture being touched by God?

# 28. Shadow and Reality

*Hebrews 8:1-8, 13*

*¹The point of what we are saying is this: We do have such a high priest, who sat down at the right hand of the throne of the Majesty in heaven, ²and who serves in the sanctuary, the true tabernacle set up by the Lord, not by man. ³Every high priest is appointed to offer both gifts and sacrifices, and so it was necessary for this one also to have something to offer. ⁴If he were on earth, he would not be a priest, for there are already men who offer the gifts prescribed by the law. ⁵They serve at a sanctuary that is a copy and shadow of what is in heaven. This is why Moses was warned when he was about to build the tabernacle: "See to it that you make everything according to the pattern shown you on the mountain." ⁶But the ministry Jesus has received is as superior to theirs as the covenant of which he is mediator is superior to the old one, and it is founded on better promises. ⁷For if there had been nothing wrong with that first covenant, no place would have been sought for another. ⁸But God found fault with the people and said: "The time is coming, declares the Lord, when I will make a new covenant with the house of Israel and with the house of Judah." ¹³By calling this covenant "new", he has made the first one obsolete; and what is obsolete and ageing will soon disappear.*

*Hebrews 9:23-10:1*

*²³It was necessary, then, for the copies of the heavenly things to be purified with these sacrifices, but the heavenly things themselves with better sacrifices than these. ²⁴For Christ did not enter a man–made sanctuary that was only a copy of the true one; he entered heaven itself, now to appear for us in God's presence. ²⁵Nor did he enter heaven to offer himself again and again, the way the high priest enters the Most Holy Place every year with blood that is not his own. ²⁶Then Christ would have had to suffer many times since the creation of the world. But now he has appeared once for all at the end of the ages to do away with sin by the sacrifice of himself. [27]Just as man is destined to die once, and after that to face judgment, [28]so Christ was sacrificed once to take away the sins of many people; and he will appear a second time, not to bear sin, but to bring salvation to those who are waiting for him. [1]The law is only a shadow of the good things that are coming—not the realities themselves. For this reason it can never, by the same sacrifices repeated endlessly year after year, make perfect those who draw near to worship.*

We come to the wonderful book of Hebrews which so often sheds a new and remarkable light on the Old Testament. In Hebrews 8 the issue of the temple is considered. The writer to the Hebrews never speaks of the temple itself, but he does often speak about the tabernacle. As we have seen, the tabernacle provided the same function as the temples of Solomon, Nehemiah and Herod. In this, all he says about the tabernacle can be taken as meaning the later temples as well. Indeed it is likely that he uses the tabernacle precisely because Law lays out the practice that needed to be followed and which was also followed in the later temples. In other words, he emphasises the tabernacle because it was the basic pattern for future temples.

And he says that it is, "a sanctuary that is a *copy and shadow* of what is heaven." This is not a one-off statement. Consider the following verses:

- "[Jesus] serves … in the *true* sanctuary." (Hebrews 8:2)
- "external regulations applying until the time of the *new* order." (Hebrews 9:10)
- "[Jesus] went through the *greater and more perfect* tabernacle that is not man-made." (Hebrews 9:11)
- "a man-made sanctuary that was only a *copy* of the true one." (Hebrews 9:24)

•"the law is only a *shadow* of the good things that are coming—not realities in themselves." (Hebrews 10:1)

Apart from the last quote (which is about the law) all refer to the tabernacle. All the statements qualify the nature of the tabernacle, saying that in some way it was only provisional. This is not only true of the tabernacle/temple. In different places in Hebrews the writer also refers to the provisional nature of the Law, the sacrifice, the priesthood, the ritual, the city/kingdom and the Promised Land. All, as described in the Old Testament, were a shadow of what God had planned and which began to be fulfilled with the coming of the Messiah.

The basis for his theology is Exodus 25:40 (and also 25:9, 26:30 and 27:8) where God shows Moses the tabernacle in the wilderness and says, "See you make everything according to the pattern shown you" (Hebrews 8:5). The word used for pattern suggests something visible and physical in front of Moses that he was to follow. It was not merely a theory but a reality that he was allowed to glimpse. The tabernacle, as described in the first part of Hebrews 9, was not perfect. All the symbolism, the detail, the beauty, even, dare one say, the abiding of the Lord himself, was not enough to make it perfect. It was only a *shadow and copy* of what he had seen.

*Shadow and copy* are perhaps the most distinctive words the writer uses to describe this. In Greek the word for *copy* is *hypodeigma*. It can mean a moral example but in this context it means a representation or delineation. In other words it is a model or a blueprint. We use the word model today for a mathematical model or a computer model, but it can equally mean an airfix model. There are a number of models today made of Herod's temple (you can see a large one in Jerusalem) and Hebrews is saying that the real temple in Jerusalem was simply a model as these small-scale models are. Equally a blueprint is a representation of the real thing but it is not the real thing. It is only a line drawing.

The Greek word for *shadow* is *skia*, and this is even more interesting. Like our word it can be used for something dark and fearful, like death, but here it simply means the image cast by an object through the sunlight hitting it. This takes up the shape of the object but it is not the object. In Colossians 2:17 Paul says about the religious festivals in the law, "these are the shadow of the things that were to come; the reality, however, is found in Christ." It is this point that the writer to the Hebrews is making. The temple in Jerusalem had no reality in itself. Its existence was dependent on the true temple, of which it was only a shadow cast by the light of God.

What then is the writer saying to the Jewish Christians nearly 2000 years ago? Simply this: the great temple in Jerusalem was not the real deal. The real deal was Jesus. The messiahship of Jesus went far beyond what any of them had imagined. The sacrifice of Jesus was in a sanctuary that was man-made. We are told he entered heaven itself. Moreover he had only to do it once, because his sacrifice was perfect. Jesus serves in a sanctuary that is perfect, because it is set up by the Lord and not man.

This vision seems far away from our matter-of-fact scientific world, but here as Christians we have a mystic heritage that is more and more attractive to those looking for spiritual answers. The temple continues, but in heaven where the one true sacrifice exists for all who want it. Jesus continues in his ministry, and it is available for us all. Yet this temple and this ministry are not simply separate from us. Although it is not in these passages from Hebrews, we know that the effects of the sacrifice can be ours today. Jesus specifically left a connection at the last supper. The bread and the wine represent his ongoing ministry in the sanctuary. His sacrifice is made real to us. Thus the true sanctuary can descend from heaven to us as we receive in faith. There is a Van Morrison song, "Queen of the Slipstream" which includes this line: "There's a dream where the contents are made visible". The Jerusalem temple, the shadow, is the image cast by the reality in heaven, but now we have a foretaste of the reality on earth. This is why the physical temple in Jerusalem is redundant. Who wants the shadow when the real thing is available?

Nevertheless there is a sense that we still live in the shadow. Until the return of Jesus and the temple from heaven, we can never know the fullness of the reality. C. S. Lewis, in his final "Narnia" book, "The Last Battle" also spoke of the difference between shadow and reality. He was speaking of heaven and earth but, as we have seen, this is anyway closely connected with the temple.

"When Aslan said you could never go back to Narnia, he meant the Narnia you were thinking of. But that is not the real Narnia. That had a beginning and an end. It was only a shadow or copy of the real Narnia which has always been here and always will be here: just as our own world, England and all, is only a shadow or copy of something in Aslan's real world. You need not mourn over Narnia, Lucy. All of the old Narnia that mattered, all the dear creatures, have been drawn into the real Narnia through the Door. And of course it is different; as different as the real thing is from a shadow or as waking life is from a dream."[1]

In the same way we need not mourn the loss of the temple as the ancient Jews did, or to hope for its rebuilding. It is existent in heaven, the place of the great and permanent sacrifice where our Lord makes permanent prayers for us all.

## Questions to consider

Find something which is a pattern or copy (like a jigsaw or a photo); see how they are different from the original (perhaps listing the differences).

Pray to Jesus as he prays for us in the greater sanctuary.

Work out the differences between the old (shadow) covenant and the new (true) covenant from Hebrews 8 and 9.

---

[1] C. S. Lewis, *The Last Battle* p.153-4 The Bodley Head 1956

# 29. The Mountaintop

*Haggai 2:6-9*

> [6]*"This is what the LORD Almighty says: 'In a little while I will once more shake the heavens and the earth, the sea and the dry land.* [7]*I will shake all nations, and the desired of all nations will come, and I will fill this house with glory,' says the LORD Almighty.* [8]*'The silver is mine and the gold is mine,' declares the LORD Almighty.* [9]*'The glory of this present house will be greater than the glory of the former house,' says the LORD Almighty. 'And in this place I will grant peace,' declares the LORD Almighty."*

*Hebrews 12:14-29*

> [14]*Make every effort to live in peace with all men and to be holy; without holiness no-one will see the Lord.* [15]*See to it that no-one misses the grace of God and that no bitter root grows up to cause trouble and defile many.* [16]*See that no-one is sexually immoral, or is godless like Esau, who for a single meal sold his inheritance rights as the oldest son.* [17]*Afterwards, as you know, when he wanted to inherit this blessing, he was rejected. He could bring about no change of mind, though he sought the blessing with tears.* [18]*You have not come to a mountain that can be touched and that is burning with fire; to darkness, gloom and storm;* [19]*to a trumpet blast or to such a voice speaking words that those who heard it begged that no further word be spoken to them,* [20]*because they could not bear what was commanded: "If even an animal touches the mountain, it must be stoned."* [21]*The sight was so terrifying that Moses said, "I am trembling with fear."* [22]*But you have come to Mount Zion, to the heavenly Jerusalem, the city of the living God. You have come to thousands upon thousands of angels in joyful assembly,* [23]*to the church of the firstborn, whose names are written in heaven. You have come to God, the judge of all men, to the spirits of righteous men made*

*perfect, [24]to Jesus the mediator of a new covenant, and to the sprinkled blood that speaks a better word than the blood of Abel. [25]See to it that you do not refuse him who speaks. If they did not escape when they refused him who warned them on earth, how much less will we, if we turn away from him who warns us from heaven? [26]At that time his voice shook the earth, but now he has promised, "Once more I will shake not only the earth but also the heavens." [27]The words "once more" indicate the removing of what can be shaken—that is, created things—so that what cannot be shaken may remain. [28]Therefore, since we are receiving a kingdom that cannot be shaken, let us be thankful, and so worship God acceptably with reverence and awe, [29]for our "God is a consuming fire."*

"Straight ahead, across a wide lake of darkness dotted with tiny fire, there was a great burning glow; and from it rose in huge columns a swirling smoke, dusky red at the roots, black above where it merged into the billowing canopy that roofed all the accursed land. (He) was looking at…the Mountain of Fire." [1]

S am's view of the mountain of doom in the Lord of the Rings could have come straight from Hebrews, "a mountain that is burning with fire; darkness, gloom and storm…". In fact it is quite possible that this incident written about in Hebrews and Exodus inspired the writings of Tolkien. The majesty of God meeting Moses on the mountain in Exodus is overwhelming, as the writer to the Hebrews is keen to point out, and Tolkien wants to create the same impression. However there is one essential difference: Mount Doom in the Lord of the Rings is completely evil, whereas Mount Sinai in Exodus is completely holy.

The word to use of the mountain is "holy" rather than "good" (although it is this as well) because the experience of God is his utter separateness and perfection, so that the mountain on which

---

[1] J. R. R. Tolkien, *The Return of the King*, p. 175 George Allen and Unwin, 1955

he appeared is transformed. It was clouded with fire, smoke and storm to the extent that an unclean creature only touching it would be destroyed. The holiness of God is such that he is completely inaccessible unless he himself (as he did with Moses) allows himself to be made accessible.

Our casualness with God as Christians is very damaging. We need to have a whole vision of God before we realise the great privilege we have in being able to come close to him. His glory is overwhelming, but there is nothing remotely bad in his majesty. The God of the Old Testament is often contrasted with the God of the New as though they were somehow different. In fact it is one and the same God and his holiness remains undimmed. Mount Sinai remains a prototype for the temple because of the presence of God and his laying down the plans for the tabernacle on that occasion that had to be constructed. The holiness of God, in smoke and fire, filled the temple. Hebrews says it was an occasion to tremble with fear, a reference to Moses words in Deuteronomy. 9:19. This is the reality of the God we worship. Some have blasphemously compared him to a puffed up tyrant who executes and kills at a whim. The truth rather is that he is genuinely so majestic and holy that we should know our place and trust and obey him. Sanity and life lay in nothing else.

However there is a great change between the two Testaments, as the writer to the Hebrews is keen to point out. It is not in the nature of God but in the action of God. We have come to another mountain, Mount Zion. It cannot be touched—yet—because it is still above. However the day will come when it is possible to touch the mountain and be in full communion with this almighty and holy God. Mount Zion is contrasted deliberately with Mount Sinai. Here is the heavenly Jerusalem, the city of God. The Israelites in the desert could not even approach the mountain. Now there is a city on the mountain, populated by thousands and thousands of angels and "the spirits of righteous men made perfect" (presumably a reference to the heroes of faith before Christ listed in chapter 11 of Hebrews). In amongst the great and the angels is the church of the firstborn, whose names are written in heaven. Who are these? Jesus said, "Rejoice that your names are written in heaven" (Luke 10:20).

Thus all people born in Christ are enrolled into the great assembly. To underline the point we are told that we, the readers, have come to God, the judge of all men. We are on the mountain.

How can this be? It is because we have not only come to the judge of all men but also to Jesus, the mediator of the new covenant. Here we once more enter the language of the temple, of blood sacrifice (better than the blood of Abel) that allows us to be present. Jesus went to Mount Zion, this time the earthly one, and there gave his blood to allow us access for eternity into the temple and the presence of God. The writer to the Hebrews quotes the prophet Haggai, where he says, "This is what the LORD Almighty says: 'In a little while I will once more shake the heavens and the earth, the sea and the dry land. I will shake all nations, and the desired of all nations will come, and I will fill this house with glory,' says the LORD Almighty". The point is this: the shaking has happened, and the unshakable kingdom has been established. We are part of this kingdom where God has filled his temple and the mountain is now unshakable.

It is the desire of many of us to reach the mountaintop of God. Indeed the phrase, "go to the mountaintop" has become synonymous with a wonderful religious experience, or even in common parlance a secular one. This passage tells us that we should indeed have such an ambition. As it says, "See to it that you do not refuse him who speaks. If they did not escape when they refused him who warned them on earth, how much less will we, if we turn away from him who warns us from heaven?" However we would be unwise to see the mountaintop as an entirely easy place this side of heaven. It is the place of God, and the living God often has a calling for his children that is hard as well as uplifting. Moses saw the Promised Land from a mountain (Mount Nebo) but he never went in. Elijah saw God work in power on the mountain confronting the prophets of Baal but then ran to Mount Sinai in depression, and his experience of God was a still, small voice. Jesus was glorified on the Mount of Transfiguration and ascended the Mount of Olives, but on both occasions the disciples were challenged as well as inspired. Jesus is our great example and his visit to Mount Zion was to be uplifted and crowned on the cross. On the day before his assassination in

1968 Martin Luther King put it like this: "We've got some difficult days ahead. But it doesn't matter with me now. Because I've been to the mountaintop. And I don't mind. Like anybody, I would like to live a long life. Longevity has its place. But I'm not concerned about that now. I just want to do God's will. And He's allowed me to go up to the mountain. And I've looked over. And I've seen the promised land. I may not get there with you. But I want you to know tonight, that we, as a people, will get to the promised land. And I'm happy, tonight. I'm not worried about anything. I'm not fearing any man. Mine eyes have seen the glory of the coming of the Lord." [1]

In Martin Luther King's case he was thanking God for the success of the civil rights movement in the U.S. in the 1960's, a cause that gave him great prominence and success but also great pain and hardship. Once we see the mountain top in that light, I think it becomes obvious that there is a mountaintop experience waiting for each one of us. This is because it is a meeting with God in his holy temple, a calling which is for all Christians. In these circumstances the mountaintop becomes one of the few experiences in one's life where we both know God very close and receive a direction that changes everything.

The experience of Frodo on Mount Doom is not too trite to use as another example. There, like Jesus, he defeated evil by sacrifice (although, unlike Jesus, he succumbed to temptation first). Thereafter he had a new calling as well as glory, a calling to a small and unimportant land. And it transpired that he could never settle, even after he had completed his calling, because his pain was too great. Rather he was relieved of his burden by going across the sea, a journey very like our own after death to the heavenly Jerusalem on Mount Zion. Here he would receive a healing experience beyond all others.

So make no mistake. There will be a greater mountaintop experience, where we will see God face to face in his temple, because of Jesus' work on Mount Zion. That is the ultimate of which all else is but a shadow. We will know God and be overpowered by love and mercy.

---

[1] Martin Luther King, *Say It Plain. A Century of Great African American Speeches.* by American Radio Works

**Questions to consider**

Look back on your life. Have you had a "mountaintop" experience of God?

Thank God for what has happened since then, and/or repent of your failing to follow the calling.

Are you at a time when you need a new direction through God's presence? Ask him to come and direct you.

Have you had such an experience of God recently? Ask him to help you in the path of following his call.

# 30. A Sacrifice of Praise

*Exodus 29:11-14*

> [11]*Slaughter it in the LORD's presence at the entrance to the Tent of Meeting.* [12]*Take some of the bull's blood and put it on the horns of the altar with your finger, and pour out the rest of it at the base of the altar.* [13]*Then take all the fat around the inner parts, the covering of the liver, and both kidneys with the fat on them, and burn them on the altar.* [14]*But burn the bull's flesh and its hide and its offal outside the camp. It is a sin offering.*

*Psalm 51: 10-19*

> [10]*Create in me a pure heart, O God, and renew a steadfast spirit within me.* [11]*Do not cast me from your presence or take your Holy Spirit from me.* [12]*Restore to me the joy of your salvation and grant me a willing spirit, to sustain me.* [13]*Then I will teach transgressors your ways, and sinners will turn back to you.* [14]*Save me from bloodguilt, O God, the God who saves me, and my tongue will sing of your righteousness.* [15]*O Lord, open my lips, and my mouth will declare your praise.* [16]*You do not delight in sacrifice, or I would bring it; you do not take pleasure in burnt offerings.* [17]*The sacrifices of God are a broken spirit; a broken and contrite heart, O God, you will not despise.* [18]*In your good pleasure make Zion prosper; build up the walls of Jerusalem.* [19]*Then there will be righteous sacrifices, whole burnt offerings to delight you; then bulls will be offered on your altar.*

*Hebrews 13: 11-16*

> [11]*The high priest carries the blood of animals into the Most Holy Place as a sin offering, but the bodies are burned outside the camp.* [12]*And so Jesus also suffered outside the city gate to make the people holy through his own blood.* [13]*Let us, then, go to him outside the camp, bearing the*

*disgrace he bore. [14]For here we do not have an enduring city, but we are looking for the city that is to come. [15]Through Jesus, therefore, let us continually offer to God a sacrifice of praise—the fruit of lips that confess his name. [16]And do not forget to do good and to share with others, for with such sacrifices God is pleased.*

*Philippians 4:18*

*[18]I have received full payment and even more; I am amply supplied, now that I have received from Epaphroditus the gifts you sent. They are a fragrant offering, an acceptable sacrifice, pleasing to God.*

*Romans 12: 1-2*

*[1]Therefore, I urge you, brothers, in view of God's mercy, to offer your bodies as living sacrifices, holy and pleasing to God—this is your spiritual act of worship. [2]Do not conform any longer to the pattern of this world, but be transformed by the renewing of your mind. Then you will be able to test and approve what God's will is—his good, pleasing and perfect will.*

Definition of sacrifice (1): "a ritual killing of a person or animal with the intention of propitiating or pleasing a deity"[1].

One of the great wonders of the ancient world is Petra in Jordan. It is a magnificent sight, approached through a narrow gorge called the *Siq* (you may have seen it in Indiana Jones and the Last Crusade) that made it virtually impregnable to attack. It also had an excellent water supply and a huge area inside to grow crops. The only way the Romans managed to defeat it was to move the trade routes so that it lost all its income. Inside Petra there is one of the few remaining intact "High Places" that are mentioned in the Bible. In this case sacrifices were made to appease the Petran gods. The High Place in Petra is nearly 200 metres above the valley floor and is approached by climbing steps cut out of the red sandstone for which Petra is famous. This High Place has survived so well

[1] *Collins English Dictionary* (third edition) 1991 HarperCollins

because it is cut out of rock itself, a level oval platform 70 metres by 20 metres, with the sanctuary in the middle. On three sides there are benches for worshippers. The altar is a raised area on the west side, and here blood sacrifices were made. One can still see the drains and basins around the altar for the blood letting that would have occurred. There is also a small pool of water to wash down the area afterwards. There is some written evidence that there were human sacrifices of boys and girls to the Petran gods, Dusares and Uzza, although undoubtedly animals were sacrificed more commonly. The blood sacrifice of an animal or a human would have brought feelings of happiness and joy at the grace given by the god in accepting the sacrifice. Blood was the symbol and source of life, and it properly belonged to the god as far as the people were concerned. In sacrificing, and then sprinkling the blood over the people and their property, there was a renewal of the relationship between man and the god.

We shudder today at the thought of such a sacrifice, especially a human one. We are probably mainly informed by the Hollywood images of unwilling western maidens being sacrificed by savages to an equally savage god (King Kong perhaps comes to mind!). However ancient people were not as foolish as that. In their sacrificial rites, such as at Petra, they were doing the greatest service they could imagine and receiving the greatest blessing possible. The human sacrificial victim would have gone willingly, perhaps even joyfully, to death. One Nabatean inscription at Hegra (some way from Petra) reads: Abd-Wadd, priest of Wadd, and his son Salim, and Zayd-Wadd, have consecrated the young man Salim to be immolated to Dhu Gabat. Their double happiness."

We condemn the ancient practices as being against what our God wants but, if we are to understand, we also need to empathise with what was going on. There was a deep desire not just to appease a deity but to be at one with him or her. There was a hope for a blessing. We can learn from their sacrifices and practices because our God demands something similar (and also something very dissimilar). Our God indeed demands our lives as a free will offering. The real difference is in the nature of our God. He gives himself instead of us and he desires justice and not blood sacrifice from us. I am sure Abd-Wadd, the priest who sacrificed his son to the god Dhu Gabat those many centuries ago, would have been pleased to know that God loves us so much he was willing to sacrifice his own son instead of Salim.

Definition of sacrifice (2): "a surrender of something of value as a means of gaining something more desirable or preventing some evil[1].

There is another definition of sacrifice that this time is essentially self-centred. You can see it in a chess game. In chess you can sacrifice your pawn in the opening (that is to say, you deliberately let your opponent take the pawn without immediate recompense) knowing full well that in due course you can take a more valuable piece or force a checkmate. In other words the sacrifice is not real; it is simply a temporary manoeuvre in the hope of getting something better. This happens in most religious life and goes something like this: "God, I promise to give up smoking if you will only let my sister recover from her illness". This is the kind of bargain we sometimes try to make with God. Because our God is a God of grace he sometimes answers those prayers. However he does not answer them because of the sacrifice we made. Rather he loves us and wants to encourage us, and in his grace he will start where we are. It is not the kind of sacrifice that we find commanded in the Bible. In this case the giving up is real but temporary, it has a wrong view of God and it comes from a bargaining, rather than a sacrificial, heart. So let me give a third definition, this time my own, which did not occur in my dictionary.

Definition of sacrifice (3): "the free gift of an act of love to a friend or in worship of God".

In the Bible we find that the original sacrifices were blood sacrifices and crop sacrifices in the temple. The blood sacrifices were of animals (never of humans, as that was abhorrent to God

---

[1] *Collins English Dictionary* (third edition) 1991 HarperCollins

who made us in his image) and all sacrifices were a genuine giving up of what was valuable to the giver. They were the first fruits, whether animals or crops, and they were to be given from a thankful heart. There was a tradition that part of the offering had to be burnt outside the camp. As we move on through the Bible we find an increasing emphasis that the sacrifice God loves is of the heart as well as the gift. In Psalm 51, a psalm of David, we read both. "The sacrifices of God are a broken spirit; a broken and contrite heart you will not despise." Yet David continues to speak of the sacrifice of bulls. When we get to the letter to the Hebrews we get another slant. There is explicit recognition that Jesus is the permanent blood sacrifice; no other is necessary. It was not that God simply sacrificed his own son (as the Nabatean priest did). That would make him no better than Abd-Wadd. Rather he sacrificed himself, God incarnate, even allowing himself, like the bull of old, to be sacrificed outside the temple, outside the city itself. This was a free gift of love to us that sets us free. We no longer need to make blood sacrifices, or even to make the regulation sacrifices of the temple. Rather we look back through the bread and the wine of Holy Communion to the one great sacrifice that did away with the need for any other.

So what is the sacrifice that we as Christians must make today? It is a sacrifice of praise, as both the letter to the Hebrews and most Holy Communion services make clear. It is purely one of thanksgiving, not of duty or requirement. Yet this very sacrifice of praise is a huge thing. It is not merely singing a hymn in church or repeating a liturgy that praises God. That is important but it is not enough. Our lives need to become lives of praise as we remember what God has done for us.

Like all people Christians get depressed or unhappy. It is not sinful to do that (there are often good reasons for feeling depressed). But underneath there should be a buoyancy of joy and hope that leads to praise even in the darkest hours. It is out of praise to God that we should love others. Why? Because we are made in the image of God, the one who saved us. It is out of praise of God that we are prepared to do foolish things in faith as he leads us. Why? Because he showed that in taking up one's cross is actually the way to true joy. It is out of praise to God that we are prepared to give our bodies as a living sacrifice. Why? Because we are secure in his love. We give ourselves as a sacrificial offering to God whilst alive, not as a blood sacrifice. This is praising God to the fullest.

In Romans 12 Paul deliberately gives a foolish contrast which we can easily miss in today's culture. He says that sacrifice should be living, to the glory of God. Everyone in his time knew that a sacrifice meant death. So how do we make this living sacrifice of praise? This is the secret: it is not through gritted teeth, determination or duty. It is through knowing the sacrifice of Christ as our personal salvation, and the overflowing joy from the Holy Spirit that results. If we want to be a sacrifice of praise we must simply keep our eyes fixed on Jesus, know his salvation and be grateful.

## Questions to consider

Do you feel grateful to God? If so, say or write some prayers of thanksgiving.

Meditate on the gospel passage on the cross and relate Jesus' sacrifice to yourself.

Ask the Holy Spirit to come into your life to make you more joyful.

# 31. Ezekiel's Vision

*Ezekiel 40:1-5*

> [1]*In the twenty-fifth year of our exile, at the beginning of the year, on the tenth of the month, in the fourteenth year after the fall of the city—on that very day the hand of the LORD was upon me and he took me there. [2]In visions of God he took me to the land of Israel and set me on a very high mountain, on whose south side were some buildings that looked like a city. [3]He took me there, and I saw a man whose appearance was like bronze; he was standing in the gateway with a linen cord and a measuring rod in his hand. [4]The man said to me, "Son of man, look with your eyes and hear with your ears and pay attention to everything I am going to show you, for that is why you have been brought here. Tell the house of Israel everything you see." [5]I saw a wall completely surrounding the temple area. The length of the measuring rod in the man's hand was six long cubits, each of which was a cubit and a handbreadth. He measured the wall; it was one measuring rod thick and one rod high.*

*Ezekiel 47:1-5*

> [1]*The man brought me back to the entrance of the temple, and I saw water coming out from under the threshold of the temple towards the east (for the temple faced east). The water was coming down from under the south side of the temple, south of the altar. [2]He then brought me out through the north gate and led me round the outside to the outer gate facing east, and the water was flowing from the south side. [3]As the man went eastward with a measuring line in his hand, he measured off a thousand cubits and then led me through water that was ankle-deep. [4]He measured off another thousand cubits and led me through water that was knee-deep. He measured off another thousand and led me through water that was up to the waist. [5]He measured off another thousand, but now it was*

*a river that I could not cross, because the water had risen and was deep enough to swim in—a river that no-one could cross.*

*Revelation 21:2-3, 10-17*

¹*Then I saw a new heaven and a new earth, for the first heaven and the first earth had passed away, and there was no longer any sea.* ²*I saw the Holy City, the new Jerusalem, coming down out of heaven from God, prepared as a bride beautifully dressed for her husband.* ³*And I heard a loud voice from the throne saying, "Now the dwelling of God is with men, and he will live with them. They will be his people, and God himself will be with them and be their God.* ¹⁰*And he carried me away in the Spirit to a mountain great and high, and showed me the Holy City, Jerusalem, coming down out of heaven from God.* ¹¹*It shone with the glory of God, and its brilliance was like that of a very precious jewel, like a jasper, clear as crystal.* ¹²*It had a great, high wall with twelve gates, and with twelve angels at the gates. On the gates were written the names of the twelve tribes of Israel.* ¹³*There were three gates on the east, three on the north, three on the south and three on the west.* ¹⁴*The wall of the city had twelve foundations, and on them were the names of the twelve apostles of the Lamb.* ¹⁵*The angel who talked with me had a measuring rod of gold to measure the city, its gates and its walls.* ¹⁶*The city was laid out like a square, as long as it was wide. He measured the city with the rod and found it to be 12,000 stadia in length, and as wide and high as it is long.* ¹⁷*He measured its wall and it was 144 cubits thick, by man's measurement, which the angel was using.*

No study of the temple can be complete without reference to the vision of Ezekiel the prophet. In chapters 40-48 of the book of Ezekiel there are in depth details of the temple he saw in a vision. It is the longest single description of the temple in the Bible. What are we to make of it?

There are three basic interpretations of his vision. One is that it is a literal description of what God will do in the rebuilding of the final temple. Because it is so detailed in its description of the measurements and structures it is sometimes assumed that there can be no other explanation. A second explanation is that it is an ideal description of the heavenly temple never intended to be established, perhaps a symbolic description of the church. Whilst there may be some truth in that, it cannot do justice to the context of the vision. A third explanation is that it is a description of a heavenly temple that will be established on earth in a way too marvellous for us to understand. This is the explanation I prefer for reasons that will become clear.

To understand this we need to understand more about the Bible. Why is Ezekiel's description not literal? Why is it not going to be built in that form in the Holy Land at the beginning of the millennium (as most millennialists believe)? The answer lies in the text of Ezekiel and in the rest of the Bible.

First of all, when we look at the introduction to the vision in chapter 40 it is very similar to the introductions to the visions in chapters 1 and 8. There is a specific date the vision occurred. There is the phrase "the hand of Yahweh came upon him". It is said that he "saw visions". (See Ezekiel 1:1-3; 8:1-3; 40:1-2) In the first vision he sees God in his glory in heaven, in the second he sees the glory depart back to heaven. The third is the continuation of this series of visions as he sees the perfect heavenly temple in heaven. Thus we are speaking of a temple in heaven, not on earth.

Secondly, at the beginning of the vision (Ezekiel 40:2) the prophet is taken to a very high mountain. The term "very high mountain" cannot be literal as there are no very high mountains around Jerusalem. Mount Zion itself is scarcely higher than the surrounding hills. Ezekiel also sees a "structure like a city" (which is a better translation than "some buildings"). This is a reference to the temple being also like a city and encompassing the whole of the holy city. Similarly at the end of the vision (Ezekiel 48:35) we hear the name of the city will be, "the Lord is there". This shows that the whole of the city will be the place of God, the temple, and that it awaits the final return of the Messiah. It is not for the present day.

Thirdly there are details in the vision which are quite impractical (alongside others, it must be said, that could be practical). As an architectural plan it makes no sense because there is no vertical scale. The boundaries of the temple are approximately the size of ancient Jerusalem, a massive expansion. The dimensions are also completely square, symbolic of perfection but not practical on a mountaintop (or a hill like Mount Zion). Then there is the river that flows from the temple. It gets progressively deeper without any tributaries entering it and then flows into the Dead Sea. Here it reverses the salinity of the Dead Sea without being affected itself. This is not natural geography! It may be possible with massive engineering works for man to construct such a temple and river, but then it would be the work of man, not God.

Fourthly there are animal sacrifices in the temple (Ezekiel 43:19). If this is a literal end-time temple it violates the principle that Christ's sacrifice is once and for all. As Hebrews 10:18 says, "Where these have been forgiven, there is no longer any sacrifice for sin". Some have suggested that the sacrifice might only be commemorative (as if Holy Communion did not exist) but Ezekiel is explicit: "These will be used as ...offerings...to make atonement." (Ezekiel 45:19) The only explanation is that the sacrifices are symbolic, and on the same basis the temple is symbolic.

Finally there are significant features of Solomon's and Herod's temples that are absent.

1. The bronze basin (or bronze sea)
2. The golden lampstand
3. The table for shewbread
4. The altar of incense
5. The veil/curtain
6. The High Priest
7. The anointing oil
8. The ark of the covenant
9. The cherubim in the Most Holy Place
10. The altar of sacrifice has changed (it is now approached from the east) and the outer courts for the women and Gentiles in Herod's temple have gone.

All these things in this list are absent because Jesus has fulfilled them. His blood has washed away sins (there is no longer need for washing). He is the light of the world (instead of the lampstand). He is the true bread (instead of the shewbread). He caused the veil to be torn because as High Priest he entered the Most Holy Place. He (and not the ark) is seated on the throne in the Most Holy Place. He has destroyed the barriers between men and women and Jews and Gentiles. All of these are looked at elsewhere in this book.

However there seems to be more going on than simple fulfilment. What is the point of an ancient temple stripped of all its furnishings? We saw earlier (chapter 11) that the three parts of the temple corresponded to the divisions of the cosmos: the physical world, the starry heavens and the invisible heavens. The loss of all separation in these three divisions means that the work of Jesus has allowed the Most Holy Place to break into the whole temple (even the whole city, as the temple is now the city and covers the area of the whole city). Now there is the complete presence of God throughout. Jesus completed a cosmic change that goes beyond a physical temple. The temple that Ezekiel saw still has vestiges of the old temple; the sacrifices are one example. This was because the prophets were given visions that made sense to the people they were witnessing to. Without this kind of context the visions would be non-sensical. Yet within the vision itself there was enough to make the contemporary hearer understand that there was a stupendous change taking place. It is only with the sacrifice of Christ on the cross that the vision can be fully appreciated.

It might seem to some that this interpretation is being untrue to a plain interpretation of scripture. I believe the precise opposite is true. God gave a progressive revelation until Jesus came and we need to see all scriptures in the light of his coming and teaching. Let me give an example. When my son was only four years old someone kindly gave me a little moped to get around on. It was only slow but it did the job. My son used to like to get up on it, put on my helmet and gloves and pretend to ride at high speed. He now has his own licence and his own bike, one of the fastest bikes he can legally own for his age. Now he is disdainful of little mopeds, preferring the sounds, looks and speed of a real motorbike. Suppose, when he was four, I had promised him an identical moped when he grew up. He would have been delighted. Today I know he would hope that I would upgrade my promise from a moped to a real motorbike. That was the heart of the promise. It was only his lack of knowledge as a four year old that made him happy with a moped. The same is true of the Bible. God gave a progressive revelation, with many pointers to the full truth. Ezekiel's vision must be seen in the light of the revelation of Christ. God has not lied in the vision showing the sacrifice of animals in the temple; Ezekiel's vision has been "upgraded" by the work of God in Christ. There is something even better.

That is not to say that Ezekiel's temple is unreal. The temple has great prominence in the book of Revelation, and the temple there has many similarities to Ezekiel's temple. John is taken up a high mountain (Revelation 21:10, Ezekiel 40:1). God dwells (literally "tabernacles") there (Revelation 21:3, Ezekiel 43:7). There are twelve gates at the compass points (Revelation 21:12-13, Ezekiel 48:31f). An angel measures it with a rod (Revelation 21:15 and throughout Ezekiel 40-48) and there are four corners (Revelation 21:16, Ezekiel 45:1-5). The glory of the Lord is apparent (Revelation 21:23, Ezekiel 43:2) and living waters flow from the temple (Revelation 22:1, Ezekiel 47:1-9). Whilst there are also differences, these similarities are striking. And John says, "I saw the Holy City, the New Jerusalem, coming down out of heaven from God" (Revelation 21:2).

The point of Ezekiel's vision for us today is to inspire us to live and worship as the vision shows a model of God with us and God to come in his fullness. The great detail of the vision tells us of the perfection of God (seen through the detail of the perfection of the building), the justice of God (seen in the laws of the temple, Ezekiel 45:9-14), the importance of true worship and the priesthood of believers, and the need to be "circumcised in heart" (Ezekiel 44:9). The point is to see what Jesus has done in making that vision real for each one of us, and how he will complete it when he returns in glory.

**Questions to consider**

Reflect on what is missing from Ezekiel's temple and how Jesus has fulfilled them.

Try to imagine a situation where we are fully in the presence of God. How would you describe it?

In the end, is this vision scary or hopeful for you? Try to feel your emotions and prayerfully work out why you feel them.

# 32. Measuring the Temple

*Ezekiel 40:5-6, 17, 19*

> [5]*I saw a wall completely surrounding the temple area. The length of the measuring rod in the man's hand was six long cubits, each of which was a cubit and a handbreadth. He measured the wall; it was one measuring rod thick and one rod high.* [6]*Then he went to the gate facing east. He climbed its steps and measured the threshold of the gate; it was one rod deep.* [17]*Then he brought me into the outer court. There I saw some rooms and a pavement that had been constructed all round the court; there were thirty rooms along the pavement.* [19]*Then he measured the distance from the inside of the lower gateway to the outside of the inner court; it was a hundred cubits on the east side as well as on the north.*

*Revelation 11:1-13*

> [1]*I was given a reed like a measuring rod and was told, "Go and measure the temple of God and the altar, and count the worshippers there.* [2]*But exclude the outer court; do not measure it, because it has been given to the Gentiles. They will trample on the holy city for 42 months.* [3]*And I will give power to my two witnesses, and they will prophesy for 1,260 days, clothed in sackcloth."* [4]*These are the two olive trees and the two lampstands that stand before the Lord of the earth.* [5]*If anyone tries to harm them, fire comes from their mouths and devours their enemies. This is how anyone who wants to harm them must die.* [6]*These men have power to shut up the sky so that it will not rain during the time they are prophesying; and they have power to turn the waters into blood and to strike the earth with every kind of plague as often as they want.* [7]*Now when they have finished their testimony, the beast that comes up from the Abyss will attack them, and overpower and kill them.* [8]*Their bodies will lie in the street of the great city, which is figuratively called Sodom and Egypt, where*

*also their Lord was crucified. [9]For three and a half days men from every people, tribe, language and nation will gaze on their bodies and refuse them burial. [10]The inhabitants of the earth will gloat over them and will celebrate by sending each other gifts, because these two prophets had tormented those who live on the earth. [11]But after the three and a half days a breath of life from God entered them, and they stood on their feet, and terror struck those who saw them. [12]Then they heard a loud voice from heaven saying to them, "Come up here." And they went up to heaven in a cloud, while their enemies looked on. [13]At that very hour there was a severe earthquake and a tenth of the city collapsed. Seven thousand people were killed in the earthquake, and the survivors were terrified and gave glory to the God of heaven.*

News report: In the early morning of April 14th, 2006, Mahmoud Salah al-Din Abd al-Raziq, a Muslim, entered the church of Mar Girgis (Saint George) in Alexandria's al-Hadra district and stabbed three parishioners who had gathered for a service. Abd al-Raziq then proceeded to attack worshippers at two other churches, according to police accounts, before being arrested en route to a fourth. Nushi Atta Girgis, 78, died from his stab wounds, while several others were injured, some severely.

These terrible events in Egypt's second city were bad enough, but concerns were greatly amplified by the controversy sparked by the stabbings. On April 15th, during the funeral procession for Girgis, clashes broke out between Muslims and Christians, prompting the police to disperse the crowds by firing live ammunition into the air and using tear gas. One Muslim died, more than 40 people of both faiths were wounded and dozens more were arrested. The following day street fighting erupted once again after Christians marched down one of Alexandria's main thoroughfares bearing crosses and shouting slogans such as, "With our blood, with our souls, we sacrifice ourselves for you, O Messiah." The protest angered local Muslims who apparently felt the slogans insulted Islam. Many shops were damaged in the commotion and still more dozens of

Alexandrians were wounded in battles with riot police.

This story is only one of very many that could be told to illustrate the persecution of the church throughout the world. The church is not perfect and can react badly (one could question the wisdom of the demonstrators in this example although not their love for Christ). Nevertheless there are places where the church is persecuted for its very existence. The slogan of the demonstrators, "With our blood, with our souls, we sacrifice ourselves for you, O Messiah." could have come straight from the book of Revelation.

What has this to do with measuring the temple? Well, some would say nothing. More than any other book in the bible, our prior theology determines how we read Revelation. Revelation is the most enigmatic book in the Bible, incapable of being taken literally in every detail by anyone. (If you have any doubt about this, consider this passage: "When the dragon saw that he had been hurled to the earth, he pursued the woman that had given birth to the male child. The woman was given the two wings of a great eagle, so that she might fly to a place prepared for her in the desert, where she would be taken care of for a time, times and half a time, out of the serpent's reach." (Revelation 12:13, 14). It is impossible to believe this is all literal, especially as the book tells us that the dragon is Satan.)

Revelation is a book of symbols, of hidden meaning, of literal statements and figurative statements all put together in a way that is difficult for modern (but not ancient) readers. Revelation 11 is one of many chapters that could be chosen in Revelation to illustrate the temple and in some ways it is illustrative of the whole book.

Some would say that Revelation 11:1-4 is a literal account of the future temple in the Holy City (Jerusalem). However everything we have read and seen so far in this book points against that: the destruction of the temple and Jesus prophecy that it would be rebuilt in three days; the identification of the temple with Jesus' body and through that the church, the body of Christ; and the coming of God as Holy Spirit so that he no longer needs a place where he is specially present. Moreover the book of Revelation itself does not support a literal interpretation of these verses. Just a few verses later Jerusalem is compared to Sodom and Egypt (Revelation 11:8), not the place of the presence of God. Revelation is crucial to our understanding of God's message to us (that is why it is in the Bible), including his teaching about the temple. However it does not have to be literal to be of importance.

John is given a measuring stick and told to measure the temple of God and the altar, and to count the worshippers (but to exclude the outer court). Ezekiel's similar vision had an angel measuring the temple. The measuring stick used both times is actually a rod or reed cut to a set length so that it could be used as a kind of ruler. John does not measure the outer court because that is the place of the Gentiles. Why is John given this task of measuring one part of the temple and not another part? The act of measuring appears to give some kind of protection and the failure to measure leaves the outer court exposed to destruction. (The word used for "temple" in this passage is actually *naos* which can be translated as the whole temple but strictly speaking only means the sanctuary in a temple, and this is what John means here. He only measures the *naos*.) How then does this image speak to us of the temple which is now Christ and his people? Let me suggest three ways, all of which are repeated in different ways throughout Revelation.

## 1] The altar

The purpose of an altar is to be a place of sacrifice. Revelation speaks of the Lamb repeatedly and "the Lamb looking as if it had been slain" (Revelation 5:6) which are obvious references to the sacrifice of Jesus on the cross. For any ancient reader the term "altar" immediately brings to mind sacrifice. Jesus identified the temple with his body but equally he was sacrificed on the day of Passover as the paschal lamb. The temple is specifically described in Revelation 11 as the "temple of God". This then is the place where God exists in his fullness. Around the altar are the worshippers whom John is also told to measure. They are a part of the temple and because they are so close to the altar they probably should be assumed to be priests. This counting of the worshippers and the protection they receive brings in another theme of Revelation: they are among those written in the Lamb's book of life (e.g. Revelation 20:12).

*2] The sanctuary*

In this pattern the sanctuary represents the living stones of the present temple who are sheltered within the protection of God for eternity. There is a part of our Christian life that is inviolate, untouchable for the evil one. This includes those Christians who have left this present life but also includes us who believe. In the grace of God, whose presence is permanently in his temple, he gives all the covering we need for eternal life.

*3] The outer court*

However the outer court is given over to the Gentiles who will trample the holy city underfoot. It could be thought that this is the world outside the church (or perhaps apostate Christians). However that is not possible because in Revelation 13:7 we see that "(Satan) was given power to make war against the saints and conquer them." The outer court signifies that part of our existence as God's people where we suffer for his sake. Persecution is allowed for a season, namely 1260 days or 42 months. This is actually the famous time scale for persecution in Daniel 7:25 (and 12:7), and again it is not meant to be literal. 42 is 7 x 6, a combination of a holy number and an unholy number. What John is doing is sending us, the reader, a signal. Whenever he uses this formula he is signifying a great persecution of the saints. God is not offering the church security from bodily suffering or death; rather we are to remain vulnerable to enmity in various forms, secure only in our faith in Jesus who was sacrificed on the altar and rose again.

In the midst of this suffering are two witnesses, described as olive trees and oil lamps, who are given power to witness about Jesus. Who are these witnesses? Once again John is using symbols. There is disagreement over exactly who they are but because they are described as prophets (v.10) they probably represent Moses and Elijah who appeared to Jesus at the transfiguration. In this way they represent not only the witness of the law and the prophets but also the totality of Christian witness. They are, if you like, the whole of the true witness that believers will give.

They will have the power of God for a time (v.4-7) but then they will be conquered and killed. For three and a half days (instead of three and a half years in verses 2 and 3) they will lie abandoned but then they will revive and ascend to God (v.12). For those in the city there will be judgment by earthquake but then a time of repentance for those who remain (v.13).

This shows us a little how the book of Revelation works, because after the measuring of the temple we get the witness of the prophets and the story is essentially very similar: a protection, a persecution (for a similar amount of time) and then redemption. Revelation does not go forward in a straight line but in reinforcing circles.

This is not our normal experience as western Christians but it may well be coming. Revelation is a stunning mixture of past, present and future, and it applies for Christians today. Persecution is a normal experience for most Christians. When we see our brothers and sisters in Alexandria attacked the week before Easter, in what was a fairly minor attack for Egypt, we are seeing this measuring of the temple in process. They were attacked for their faith, and their response was, "With our blood, with our souls, we sacrifice ourselves for you, O Messiah." There is little doubt that the marginalisation and oppression of Christians for their faith is rising in Britain today. There are examples of deliberate misrepresentation in the media; there are national laws in direct contravention of the Ten Commandments; there are laws which, as they are applied more rigorously, may lead to obedient Christians being harassed at work or even sacked. Yet we must not fool ourselves. Some of this criticism and difficulty being experienced by the church in Britain is due to our foolishness or sinfulness, particularly our own hypocrisy and sexual sins. The time of persecution is not quite here yet.

Revelation is undoubtedly a difficult book and it requires careful explanation. But as we study these verses we see a rich theme: we, the Church, are the place of Christ and the reason why he died. God dwells in us and we are called to worship him and witness to him. There is not total protection from the evils of this world until we finally meet him in fullness, which will either be in our death or his return.

**Questions to consider**
Look at the example of the Egyptian Christians.
Did they react in a Christ-like way?
How was their witness true, and how did it fail?
What would you do if someone killed a church friend of yours simply because they were a Christian and then the state protected the murderer?
Are you oppressed as a Christian today? How can you love those who hate or dislike you?

# 33. The Antichrist in the Temple

*2 Thessalonians 2:1-17*

<sup>1</sup>*Concerning the coming of our Lord Jesus Christ and our being gathered to him, we ask you, brothers,* <sup>2</sup>*not to become easily unsettled or alarmed by some prophecy, report or letter supposed to have come from us, saying that the day of the Lord has already come.* <sup>3</sup>*Don't let anyone deceive you in any way, for that day will not come until the rebellion occurs and the man of lawlessness is revealed, the man doomed to destruction.* <sup>4</sup>*He will oppose and will exalt himself over everything that is called God or is worshipped, so that he sets himself up in God's temple, proclaiming himself to be God.* <sup>5</sup>*Don't you remember that when I was with you I used to tell you these things?* <sup>6</sup>*And now you know what is holding him back, so that he may be revealed at the proper time.* <sup>7</sup>*For the secret power of lawlessness is already at work; but the one who now holds it back will continue to do so till he is taken out of the way.* <sup>8</sup>*And then the lawless one will be revealed, whom the Lord Jesus will overthrow with the breath of his mouth and destroy by the splendour of his coming.* <sup>9</sup>*The coming of the lawless one will be in accordance with the work of Satan displayed in all kinds of counterfeit miracles, signs and wonders,* <sup>10</sup>*and in every sort of evil that deceives those who are perishing. They perish because they refused to love the truth and so be saved.* <sup>11</sup>*For this reason God sends them a powerful delusion so that they will believe the lie* <sup>12</sup>*and so that all will be condemned who have not believed the truth but have delighted in wickedness.* <sup>13</sup>*But we ought always to thank God for you, brothers loved by the Lord, because from the beginning God chose you to be saved through the sanctifying work of the Spirit and through belief in the truth.* <sup>14</sup>*He called you to this through our gospel, that you might share in the glory of our Lord Jesus Christ.* <sup>15</sup>*So then, brothers, stand firm and hold to the teachings we passed*

*on to you, whether by word of mouth or by letter. ¹⁶May our Lord Jesus Christ himself and God our Father, who loved us and by his grace gave us eternal encouragement and good hope, ¹⁷encourage your hearts and strengthen you in every good deed and word.*

*Revelation 13:5-10*

*⁵The beast was given a mouth to utter proud words and blasphemies and to exercise his authority for forty-two months. ⁶He opened his mouth to blaspheme God, and to slander his name and his dwelling-place and those who live in heaven. ⁷He was given power to make war against the saints and to conquer them. And he was given authority over every tribe, people, language and nation. ⁸All inhabitants of the earth will worship the beast—all whose names have not been written in the book of life belonging to the Lamb that was slain from the creation of the world. ⁹He who has an ear, let him hear. ¹⁰ If anyone is to go into captivity, into captivity he will go. If anyone is to be killed with the sword, with the sword he will be killed. This calls for patient endurance and faithfulness on the part of the saints.*

Antiochus IV Epiphanes was a descendant of Alexander the Great. He took over a part of Alexander's empire in 175 B.C.. He was a brutal man who persecuted the Jews ruthlessly (you can read more about the story in the apocryphal books of Maccabees). In Jerusalem we read he killed over 40,000 men, women and children and sold the same number into slavery (2 Maccabees 5:11-14). He went to the temple in Jerusalem, took all its treasures and dedicated it to the Greek God Jupiter Olympus. He defiled the temple by deliberately sacrificing a pig on the altar (1 Maccabees 1:47) and scattering its blood all over the holy vessels. He stopped all the Jewish feasts and substituted them with drunken feasts to Bacchus, the god of wine, forcing the Jews to join in (2 Maccabees 6:7). He named himself "Epiphanes", short for theos

epiphanies, which means, "the god who appears". In other words he announced he was a god and that he was to be worshipped.

Antiochus Epiphanes was the original antichrist. He is called the abomination of desolation in Daniel 11 and 12. Jesus referred to the abomination of desolation in Matthew 24, advising people to run to the hills when he comes. Thus there is to be at least one more abomination of desolation after Antiochus. Paul speaks of the man of lawlessness (2 Thessalonians 2:3) and in his letters John also speaks of the antichrist. In 1 John 2:18,22 he says, "This is the last hour and as you have heard the antichrist is coming, even now many antichrists have come. This is how we know it is the last hour... who is the liar? It is the man who denies that Jesus is the Christ. Such a man is the antichrist—he denies the Father and the Son." In the book of Revelation John calls him the beast, whose number is 666 (Revelation 13:18). The amount of time he is given is in God's hands (v.5) and this time is symbolic 42 (i.e.6 x 7) months, the same time Daniel gave. The name we usually use today (not least in horror movies!) is antichrist, but beast, abomination of desolation and man of lawlessness all speak of the same thing.

We are in the last times (as John says) but Jesus will not return until the antichrist comes. However, as we have seen, there are many antichrists, so identifying the last one will be difficult. We should not even try.

In the New Testament the longest treatment of the antichrist comes from Paul in 2 Thessalonians. Some of this is straightforward but some of it is more difficult. The nature of the antichrist is part of the easier teaching. He will be in rebellion against God but more than this he will set himself up as an alternative to God and especially to Jesus. Paul says (v.9) that this will be in the temple itself, "the coming of the lawless one will be in accordance to with the work of Satan displayed in all sorts of counterfeit miracles, signs and wonders, and in every sort of evil that deceives those who are perishing." How is all this to happen and what is its relevance today?

When Paul wrote the temple in Jerusalem had not yet been destroyed and the "abomination of desolation" predicted by Jesus had not yet happened. Rather as Antiochus Epiphanes fulfilled Daniel's prophecy, Jesus prophecy was fulfilled by Titus, the future

Roman Emperor, who desecrated the temple. At that time, AD 70, remembering their Lord's words, the Christians in Jerusalem fled to the hills for safety. However Paul's term "God's temple" (2 Thessalonians. 2:4) almost always means the body of Christ in the New Testament. Only once does it refer to the physical temple in Jerusalem. When Paul writes in v.3 of rebellion (apostasy or falling away) of all things godly and then tells the Thessalonians to stand firm (v.15) he is speaking about the body of believers who make up Christ's body, the true temple. Paul is speaking to the followers of Jesus so that they will not be deceived about his return. The whole purpose is to encourage the church and to give predictions of the shape (not the timing) of what will happen.

This can be summarised as follows. There will be many antichrists but ultimately there will be one who will cause great suffering before Jesus returns. He is being held back for the present until the time is right but he (or perhaps she?) will put himself in the place of God and will desecrate the true worship of Jesus' followers. There will be terrible suffering whilst he reigns but the faithful will be saved by Jesus.

It is sometimes difficult to imagine ourselves in such a position (at least, it is for western Christian; many other Christians in Islamic and Communist countries have not needed to imagine in the last 100 years). We might say, "I would not be one of those seduced away from the true faith". Let me give two examples of 20th century antichrists to show how easy it is to be deceived. (By the way it was once fashionable to call religious leaders who some believed to have gone astray as "antichrist", for example the Pope and Henry VIII. By definition antichrist is someone who takes the place of Christ. Bad and misguided leaders may show some of the attributes of the antichrist, but unless they attempt to get people to worship them they are not antichrist and certainly not the final antichrist).

Adolf Hitler, who was evil in many ways, can also with justice be called antichrist. Nazism was a religious movement as well as political. It was the redeeming movement for Germany, fighting the "satans" of communism and war reparations following the First World War. The whole movement dripped with religious imagery: the singing, parades, uniforms, architecture and the symbol of the bent cross (stolen, ironically, from Eastern religions not Christianity). Heading this essentially pagan political movement was Hitler himself who became the focus for adulation. It is easy to say now that National Socialism was unchristian but at the time many Christians were misled. They were deceived by their own weaknesses: their racism and anti-semitism (both hundreds of years old); their bitterness and nationalism after WWI; and their fear over communism. These same conditions could have prevailed easily in Britain or France if they had lost World War 1. There grew a German Christian movement that praised both Jesus and Hitler and proclaimed an aggressive Christianity. In 1944 the theologian Walter Grundmann saw the Third Reich at war as a parable for the Kingdom of God, with the Madonna with child as a symbol for the holy German motherhood and the cross the symbol of the sacrificial death of the soldiers. Hitler himself was no Christian but used the cult of adulation around him to penetrate the church. Not all German Christians succumbed. There was a struggle against Nazism, especially by Catholics and some Protestants such as Niemoller and Bonhoeffer, who called Hitler antichrist. Nevertheless as the war progressed these were a remnant who were often martyred. The beast was inside the temple.

A second example is Jim Jones and the Peoples Temple Full Gospel Church of Indianapolis and later Jonestown, Guyana. Jones became a preacher in the 1950's and was ordained in 1964. His church was renowned for its equal treatment of African Americans and for pursuing social justice. It grew. There were over 1,000 who moved to Guyana when there were attacks against the church for tax evasion and other more serious charges. The group had moved away from normal Christian faith. Jones attacked the Bible and then claimed to be the incarnation of Jesus, Akhenaten, Buddha, Lenin and Father Divine. In 1978 the church was investigated in Guyana by a U.S. representative who was then murdered. Jones committed suicide with the rest of the church shortly afterwards, although some escaped from his psychological control earlier. Although a much less extensive example than Hitler, Jones shows similar traits of antichrist. There was the desire to be god-like and to control large numbers of people in the church, beginning with their weakness and eventually destroying all that is truly Christian. This is antichrist, as by the end Christ is no longer at the centre or even the periphery of his temple; antichrist has taken his place.

Can this happen to us? The answer is yes! The final Antichrist will come and all churches, all denominations and all Christian countries face the danger. We are spiritually arrogant if we do not take seriously the warnings of scripture and the failure of other Christians in history. How do we prevent this happening? It is too late to try and resist an antichrist at the last moment. Like a student revising for an exam, the real work is done in the years before, not in the revision. To resist an antichrist we must be trained in advance. Antichrist gains entrance among the faithful by working on certain fears, prejudices and beliefs so that others are forgotten. The Germans and Americans in my examples were not so different from us.

We need to have a thorough knowledge of the scriptures as this gives us God's authority separate from man's. Yet, because the antichrist will manipulate scripture, we also need to have a sound knowledge of past interpretation of scripture. We need to have our obedience in the commands of Christ as antichrist will inevitably give other commands. Yet, because antichrist will inevitably wrap his commands up as being godly we need to understand the purposes of the will of God in his creation. We need to have good links with Christians of other traditions and not be too narrow in our faith as such narrowness can be seduced on the particular points of difference. Yet at the same time antichrist may attempt to seduce by a pan-church movement and we must beware unity as an alternative god. We need to pray but even prayer can be seduced. We need to ensure our prayer is to the suffering Christ as the antichrist will inevitably desire power. Above all then our resistance to antichrist will be in knowing the true Christ and being known by him who is, in the end, our only protector. As Paul says, "Stand firm, and hold on to the teachings passed on to you". How else can we be faithful?

## Questions to consider

How might an antichrist tempt you?
How might an antichrist get access into your denomination?
Are you prepared for a possible persecution of your faith?

# 34. The Martyrs Worship

*Revelation 7:1-17*

<sup>1</sup>*After this I saw four angels standing at the four corners of the earth, holding back the four winds of the earth to prevent any wind from blowing on the land or on the sea or on any tree.* <sup>2</sup>*Then I saw another angel coming up from the east, having the seal of the living God. He called out in a loud voice to the four angels who had been given power to harm the land and the sea:* <sup>3</sup>*"Do not harm the land or the sea or the trees until we put a seal on the foreheads of the servants of our God."* <sup>4</sup>*Then I heard the number of those who were sealed: 144,000 from all the tribes of Israel.* <sup>5</sup>*From the tribe of Judah 12,000 were sealed, from the tribe of Reuben 12,000, from the tribe of Gad 12,000,* <sup>6</sup>*from the tribe of Asher 12,000, from the tribe of Naphtali 12,000, from the tribe of Manasseh 12,000,* <sup>7</sup>*from the tribe of Simeon 12,000, from the tribe of Levi 12,000, from the tribe of Issachar 12,000,* <sup>8</sup>*from the tribe of Zebulun 12,000, from the tribe of Joseph 12,000, from the tribe of Benjamin 12,000.*

<sup>9</sup>*After this I looked and there before me was a great multitude that no-one could count, from every nation, tribe, people and language, standing before the throne and in front of the Lamb. They were wearing white robes and were holding palm branches in their hands.* <sup>10</sup>*And they cried out in a loud voice: "Salvation belongs to our God, who sits on the throne, and to the Lamb."* <sup>11</sup>*All the angels were standing round the throne and around the elders and the four living creatures. They fell down on their faces before the throne and worshipped God,* <sup>12</sup>*saying: "Amen! Praise and glory and wisdom and thanks and honour and power and strength be to our God for ever and ever. Amen!"*

<sup>13</sup>*Then one of the elders asked me, "These in white robes— who are they, and where did they come from?"* <sup>14</sup>*I answered, "Sir, you know." And he said, "These are they who have*

come out of the great tribulation; they have washed their robes and made them white in the blood of the Lamb. [15]Therefore, "they are before the throne of God and serve him day and night in his temple; and he who sits on the throne will spread his tent over them. [16] Never again will they hunger; never again will they thirst. The sun will not beat upon them, nor any scorching heat. [17] For the Lamb at the centre of the throne will be their shepherd; he will lead them to springs of living water. And God will wipe away every tear from their eyes."

*Revelation 14:1-5*

[1]Then I looked, and there before me was the Lamb, standing on Mount Zion, and with him 144,000 who had his name and his Father's name written on their foreheads. [2]And I heard a sound from heaven like the roar of rushing waters and like a loud peal of thunder. The sound I heard was like that of harpists playing their harps. [3]And they sang a new song before the throne and before the four living creatures and the elders. No-one could learn the song except the 144,000 who had been redeemed from the earth. [4]These are those who did not defile themselves with women, for they kept themselves pure. They follow the Lamb wherever he goes. They were purchased from among men and offered as firstfruits to God and the Lamb. [5]No lie was found in their mouths; they are blameless.

In 2003 this letter was sent to Christian families all over Iraq:

*'By the name of God the most merciful and compassionate!*
*"Do not adorn yourselves as illiterate women before Islam."*
*From the leadership of Islamic troops of "Al-Bader"*
*To this noble family:*
*We hope that the head of this family will stand with the "brothers of Muslims" group and follow basic Muslim rules of wearing the veil and possessing honourable teaching of Islam that Moslems have continued from old epoch. We are the Iraqi people, the Muslim people that do not accept any mistakes.*

*If not—and the message will not be followed, we will take the actions of:*
*1. Killing.*
*2. Kidnapping.*
*3. Burning the house with its occupants or exploding it.* [1]

For many Iraqi Christians the invasion of Iraq and the subsequent breakdown of government control has meant this kind of persecution. On 31st October 2010 fifty-eight Chaldean Catholics were killed in Baghdad after Islamic militants took them hostage during the Sunday service. It is not only Iraq. Today throughout the world under extreme Islam or communism or other repressive governments Christians are being martyred because they are Christians. Martyrdom not only happened when the Christians were thrown to the lions; it is estimated that more Christians were killed for their faith in the twentieth century than in any other preceding century.

In Revelation 14 John has a vision of the Lamb of God standing on Mount Zion. He is on the holy mountain which is in the holy city and symbolically at the place of sacrifice, the temple. The scene set before John is remarkable. He sees 144,000 people with the name of the Lamb and his Father written on their foreheads. To even have the name of God written at all by humans was blasphemous for many Jews. Therefore to have it written on a person by God speaks of their complete holiness and perfection. The next five or six verses go on to describe who these people are and what they are doing.

However first we need to go back a little to consider more about the book of Revelation. One way of looking at Revelation is to see John has given us an extended exposition of Psalm 2. In that Psalm the nations and their kings will conspire together, but God will install his chosen one on Zion, his holy hill, where he will conquer the heathen kings. A similar story is told in chapters 13 and 14 of Revelation (and elsewhere in Revelation). Of course John is writing after Jesus and so knows the outworking of Psalm 2: the chosen one, Jesus, conquered on Mount Zion through the cross and the resurrection and the heathen rulers Herod and Pilate were thwarted. Throughout Revelation John

---

[1] Glen Chancy in *http://www.lewrockwell.com/orig3/chancy3.html*

is insistent that the victory is shared with his followers. This brings us back to the 144,000. Who are they?

The 144,000 are also mentioned in Revelation 7, this time explicitly in the temple. As we saw before, John's writing is rather circular, or perhaps like a spiral. After a while he will return to the same subject to expound it further. So it is with chapters 7 and 14. In chapter 7 there are four angels holding back the winds of the earth, which are the winds of death and destruction (another image John uses for this are the four horsemen). They are held back until a seal is put on the 144,000 servants. The 144,000 are 12,000 from each of the 12 tribes of Israel (but not the whole of each tribe). John cannot mean that these are all Jews: elsewhere in the New Testament (James 1:1 and Matthew 19:28) the 12 tribes of Israel are used to describe the church. Often in Revelation John gives the church a title of Israel. Furthermore John goes on to describe the crowd of 144,000 as a great multitude that no-one could count from every tribe, nation, people and language (Revelation 7:9) standing before the Lamb and the throne. This multitude then is made up of the followers of the Lamb, Jesus, drawn from around the world.

The second thing we know about them is that they are servants of God with a seal of protection on their foreheads (Revelation 7:3). Why do they need special protection? Because they have come under great tribulation (Revelation 7:14) and are blameless, never having had a lie on their lips (Revelation 14:5). John often says that the servants are prophets (Revelation 10:7, 11:3, 11:18). Thus we can see that this multitude are the ones who stood firm and spread the message, protected for a time from the normal calamities of the world for a special end. In fact there is every reason to believe that this end is martyrdom because they follow the Lamb wherever he goes (Revelation 14:4) and their tribulation is physical death. They are protected until the time of their martyrdom, through which they have emerged victorious. There are others in the church who will be faithful and who will die for other reasons, but the martyrs are the first fruits (Revelation 14:4). Others will follow on.

Thus their third quality is victory. They are the conquerors who stand pure in white

robes washed in the blood of the Lamb waving palm branches. The association with Palm Sunday is unmistakable. Here we have that victory of Jesus fully realised. These are the conquerors after a great battle coming to the throne of their leader with battle honours. Yet it is not the kind of victory we expect. As we read Revelation it feels like an extremely violent battle is taking place between the forces of evil and the servants of God. Yet reading more closely we realise that the true nature of the battle is the cross and the martyrdom of Christians. The judgement comes solely from God and his angels. Our victory, as we follow him on earth now, comes not through a crusade in the Holy Land or a vicious war in modern Iraq but by the kind of martyrdom that has always occurred in these lands for Christians. These martyrs are pure and their purity is emphasised by their celibacy and truthfulness (Revelation 14:4,5). Once again this does not have to be literal: not all martyrs were celibate! John is using symbolic language to emphasise their holiness. They are worthy sacrifices themselves as they are without blemish, a purity which comes through their being washed in the blood of the Lamb.

Finally they are characterised by having a new song to sing (Revelation 14:3). We know what this song is: "Salvation belongs to our God, who sits on the throne, and to the Lamb" (Revelation 7:10) and "Amen! Praise and glory and wisdom and thanks and honour and power and strength be to our God for ever and ever. Amen!" (Revelation 7:12).

Thus we have the martyred followers of Jesus from the whole world, revealed as pure conquerors, worshipping in the temple in the place of honour. John's vision is past, present and future. The conquest is taking place but not by the means the world imagines. Judgement will come but in the meantime these conquerors will never thirst nor hunger. They will never suffer under the sun but they will receive springs of living water. God will wipe away every tear from their eyes. The vision of tenderness from the almighty to his worshippers is one of great hope. It is also one of great humility towards us.

Who is the greatest in the kingdom of heaven? We now know the answer. It is the one who follows Jesus to the cross. It is the martyr who willingly gives up his life while giving the message of the gospel to his persecutors. This is what Jesus did and this is how salvation came into being. This is what the martyrs did and are doing, and the blood of the martyrs is truly the seed of the church. For their victory (and that of Jesus) is one of salvation and not condemnation. As a result the angel of the Lord goes out with the gospel message to all the earth (Revelation 14:6).

The persecution of Iraqi Christians continues to this day. Many thousands have left their country since 2003. In all likelihood an Iraqi Christian was martyred this week without fanfare from C.N.N. or the B.B.C.. They are unheard of by the likes of us. Yet they are the true heroes of faith, not us, who may lose a church building through neglect or suffer minor indignities for our faith. We will discover that these are the ones honoured in heaven.

I began with examples of how there are modern martyrs occurring in Iraq. Let me end with some martyrs from 111-113 AD, about 20 years after John was writing and the kind of people he was writing to in his environment to encourage as they were being martyred. Here Pliny, the governor of Pontus/Bithynia (part of modern Turkey) is writing a report to the Emperor Trajan:

"Meantime this is the course I have taken with those who were accused before me as Christians. I asked them whether they were Christians, and if they confessed, I asked them a second and third time with threats of punishment. If they kept to it, I ordered them for execution; for I held no question that whatever it was that they admitted, in any case obstinacy and unbending perversity deserve to be punished. There were others of the like insanity; but as these were Roman citizens, I noted them down to be sent to Rome."[1]

Pliny was a good administrator doing his job. This meant he became the persecutor of the witnessing, faithful children of God. These are the ones whose tears God wipes away and who are hailed as conquerors.

## Questions to consider

Can you imagine yourself in such a position?
How would you react?
Why do people like Pliny and the Islamic troops of al-Bader persecute?

---

[1] Edwin M. Yamauchi, *"Harpers World of the New Testament"* New York: Lion Publishing p. 79

# 35. Judgement from the Temple

*Revelation 15:1-8*

[1]*I saw in heaven another great and marvellous sign: seven angels with the seven last plagues—last, because with them God's wrath is completed. [2]And I saw what looked like a sea of glass mixed with fire and, standing beside the sea, those who had been victorious over the beast and his image and over the number of his name. They held harps given them by God [3]and sang the song of Moses the servant of God and the song of the Lamb: "Great and marvellous are your deeds, Lord God Almighty. Just and true are your ways, King of the ages. [4] Who will not fear you, O Lord, and bring glory to your name? For you alone are holy. All nations will come and worship before you, for your righteous acts have been revealed." [5]After this I looked and in heaven the temple, that is, the tabernacle of the Testimony, was opened. [6]Out of the temple came the seven angels with the seven plagues. They were dressed in clean, shining linen and wore golden sashes round their chests. [7]Then one of the four living creatures gave to the seven angels seven golden bowls filled with the wrath of God, who lives for ever and ever. [8]And the temple was filled with smoke from the glory of God and from his power, and no-one could enter the temple until the seven plagues of the seven angels were completed.*

*Revelation 20:11 – 21:8*

[11]*Then I saw a great white throne and him who was seated on it. Earth and sky fled from his presence, and there was no place for them. [12]And I saw the dead, great and small, standing before the throne, and books were opened. Another book was opened, which is the book of life. The dead were judged according to what they had done as recorded in the books. [13]The sea gave up the dead that were in it, and death and Hades gave up the dead that were in them, and each*

*person was judged according to what he had done. [14]Then death and Hades were thrown into the lake of fire. The lake of fire is the second death. [15]If anyone's name was not found written in the book of life, he was thrown into the lake of fire. [1]Then I saw a new heaven and a new earth, for the first heaven and the first earth had passed away, and there was no longer any sea. [2]I saw the Holy City, the new Jerusalem, coming down out of heaven from God, prepared as a bride beautifully dressed for her husband. [3]And I heard a loud voice from the throne saying, "Now the dwelling of God is with men, and he will live with them. They will be his people, and God himself will be with them and be their God. [4]He will wipe every tear from their eyes. There will be no more death or mourning or crying or pain, for the old order of things has passed away." [5]He who was seated on the throne said, "I am making everything new!" Then he said, "Write this down, for these words are trustworthy and true." [6]He said to me: "It is done. I am the Alpha and the Omega, the Beginning and the End. To him who is thirsty I will give to drink without cost from the spring of the water of life. [7]He who overcomes will inherit all this, and I will be his God and he will be my son. [8]But the cowardly, the unbelieving, the vile, the murderers, the sexually immoral, those who practise magic arts, the idolaters and all liars—their place will be in the fiery lake of burning sulphur. This is the second death."*

The Middle East is used to judgement from rulers and potentates. In 1982 Hafez al-Assad, the president of Syria, ruthlessly suppressed an uprising of Islamists in Hama, a city north of Damascus. Around 25,000 were killed (no-one knows the exact number) by systematically destroying the Old City, in part by running tanks over the old buildings and crushing people underneath. In Iraq Saddam Hussein suppressed the Shi'ite marsh Arabs in their rebellion by draining their marshes and sending in the tanks. He suppressed the Kurdish rebellion in the north by using poison gas (repeating the British action in the 1920s). Israel invaded Lebanon and bombed Beirut mercilessly in 1982, killing untold numbers. Similarly Israel wrecked Gaza in 2008/9, pouring phosphorous shells on residential areas. And so one could go on down the years, recounting a litany of ruthlessness by the powerful over the less powerful. This often means we distrust judgement and punishment of any sort, and wonder if whole scale punishment can ever be just.

Revelation 15 is the chapter that begins the Last Judgement. The angel says in Revelation 16:5, "you are just in these judgements... the Holy One". We need to begin by saying that God is not just like any human ruler. The ruthlessness of modern Middle Eastern rulers is not like God. God is holy and his judgements emanate from his temple (Revelation 15:6), "out of the temple came the seven angels with the seven plagues".

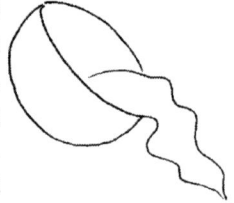

Revelation 15:1 begins with these seven angels in heaven with the seven plagues. They are unlike previous punishments in Revelation because these are the last. "With them God's wrath is completed." The vision John sees in heaven is undoubtedly exotic but it also has a familiarity. This is because much of the imagery comes from the Exodus. (Incidentally familiar symbolism is one of the great features of Revelation. Sometimes authors use symbolism to conceal but that is only to the outsider. In the main the symbolism in Revelation is meant to enhance and deepen spiritual realities, to help the worshipper come closer to God.)

To begin with we have the sea of glass. This is the sea from which the beast came (Revelation 13:1) and is a reference to Daniel 7:2-3 where four beasts come out of the sea. The sea is the place where evil lurks. (When we get to the final consummation in chapter 21 we find there is no longer any sea.) We find elsewhere in the Old Testament mention of sea monsters which will be slain by God (e.g. Psalm 74:13-14; Isaiah 51:9-10). However the great reference to sea in the Old Testament is the crossing of the Red Sea by the children of Israel in the Exodus account and the great defeat of Egypt. "Was it not you who dried up the sea?" we read in Isaiah 51:10. This is the overarching reference point to sea in the Old Testament.

The Exodus theme is at work in other ways. The martyrs, the conquerors, stand victorious on the other side of the sea, identified by their harps, They sing the song of Moses (v.3) and the tabernacle is established (v.5) filled with smoke from the glory of God and his power (v.8). This is now the true temple; it is not a shadow or a copy because (as we saw in Hebrews) this one is in heaven. Like the old tabernacle at this point no-one enters because of the glory of God, until the judgements are completed. John adds an important detail: this is the tabernacle of testimony, thus emphasising the law and judgement.

So John's vision draws on the events of the Exodus—the punishment of the Egyptians, the escape through the sea, the coming of the Law and of the tabernacle and temple—and applies it to his day and the future. The children of Israel are now the victorious martyrs who followed Jesus. The song of Moses is also the song of the Lamb. There is now the true tabernacle. This is Exodus repeated but in a final form.

Even the song of the harpists is brought from various parts of the Old Testament. It includes quotes from the Song of Moses after the Exodus (Deuteronomy 32:3) but also from the Psalms (111:2, 139:14 and 86:9) and the Prophets (Hosea 14:9, Jeremiah 10:7 and Isaiah 66:23). It is a wonderfully positive song. The greatness of God will be revealed and he will be feared and glorified. There will be true worship (and therefore we must suppose true conversion) by people from all nations. His righteousness and his justice will be apparent. We have a second Exodus, another time of judgement, redemption and glory. It is a time when justice will be supreme.

It is at this point that the angels come forth with judgement. They are dressed like pure priests (v.6) but their significance is that the time of mercy is over. This judgement is particularly to do with the persecutors, the followers of the beast (Revelation 16:2) and not all humankind (that comes later). The great martyrdom gave the persecutors the opportunity to repent but that is now ended. The first four plagues (Revelation 16:1-9) have similarities with the plagues of Egypt and the earlier trumpets plagues in Revelation, but now there is no chance for repentance. The final three are the dethronement of the beast (Revelation 16:10), the invasion of his empire (Revelation 16:13) and the destruction of his capital, "Babylon" (Revelation 16:19). Who is the oppressor, the beast?

Who are his followers? Most commentators here think that John was thinking of Rome but that he was also looking back to Pharaoh in the Exodus. However there is no need to put a specific time or application on the prophecy. John was looking past, present and future. Even so everything in these chapters point to a final judgement which will come will come like a thief (Revelation 16:15). John quotes Jesus (and Paul). These events will be sudden, unexpected and unpredictable. Despite all the detail John gives he also tells us that this vision is not designed to help us work out the times but to give us strength to persevere through them.

The next three chapters work out this judgement of the oppressors and the beast in detail. Then in Revelation 20:11-21:8 the last part of God's judgement occurs. The judgement again comes from the temple where God's throne is placed but now there is a change. Earth and heaven flee from his presence and are replaced by a new heaven and a new earth. All are judged, including the dead, according to the book before him. This is not an indiscriminate judgement, a Middle Eastern tyrant judging by tank or bombs. On the contrary, the greater book is the book of life which has individual names written in it from the creation of the world (Revelation 17:8). These individuals belong to the Lamb who was slaughtered from the creation of the world (Revelation 13:8). Here we have a sense of the omnipotence of God, who is past, present and future, and not of a lack justice for judged humanity. God is before all things so that even the sacrifice of the Lamb can be spoken of as being from the creation of the world, even though it is rooted in the history of first century Palestine. What is more it is possible for a name to be erased from that book (Revelation 3:5).

So what is the basis of God's judgement? We are told that each person is judged according to what they had done. These deeds must include seeking the forgiveness through the sacrifice of Christ. The work of the Lamb upon the cross is the ultimate basis for judgement; the whole context for this judgement is the temple and the temple sacrifice. His blood is what made forgiveness possible for even the persecutors of the martyrs. This is not a "job lot" judgement by God. Each one of us will be judged individually by him. We learn elsewhere in scripture (1 Corinthians. 3:15) that even if we are forgiven by him the deeds we have done in life will be important in that judgement. The bad will be burned away like stubble, the good refined like silver and gold. There will be true justice for everyone.

Who then is being judged? The answer is everyone, dead and alive, save the martyrs and the beast and his followers who are already judged. There is a special mention made for those who died at sea because they could not receive a proper burial. Even Hades will give up its dead. All will come before the Almighty to be judged.

So what is the result? There is a straightforward division. There are those who will suffer the "second death". They may have died already but the second death comes with the final judgement. This is the death from which there is no escape. It is the lake of fire, the symbol of everlasting destruction, of annihilation. So total is that destruction that even Hades (the waiting place of the dead) and death itself are thrown into it. Thus there will be an end to hell and death. There will also be an end to those who will not accept God's forgiveness and whose sins will lead them to destruction. They are the cowardly, the unbelieving, the vile, the murderers…whose place will be the fiery lake of destruction, the second death (Revelation 21:8). This seems unbelievably harsh to modern ears. But how can heaven be populated with unrepentant murderers? Heaven cannot be a place of disbelief or adultery; if that is the case it is no longer heaven or a place of the holiness of God. It is not that believers are intrinsically different from non-believers. Rather it is that believers are willing to turn from their evil ways and trust the Lamb for forgiveness. This is the second group, the nations who enter the new Jerusalem, whose tears are wiped away by God and who drink of the water of life.

So the judgement of God unfolds: the martyrs are justified, the beast and his followers destroyed and all other humans, dead or alive, are brought to judgement. And at the last, earth and heaven themselves are judged and there is a new heaven and a new earth. This is a true and righteous judgement.

## Question to consider

How confident are you of God's final judgement?

# 36. No Temple

*Revelation 21:1-3; 9-16; 22-22:5*

   ¹*Then I saw a new heaven and a new earth, for the first heaven and the first earth had passed away, and there was no longer any sea.* ²*I saw the Holy City, the new Jerusalem, coming down out of heaven from God, prepared as a bride beautifully dressed for her husband.* ³*And I heard a loud voice from the throne saying, "Now the dwelling of God is with men, and he will live with them. They will be his people, and God himself will be with them and be their God.*

   ⁹*One of the seven angels who had the seven bowls full of the seven last plagues came and said to me, "Come, I will show you the bride, the wife of the Lamb."* ¹⁰*And he carried me away in the Spirit to a mountain great and high, and showed me the Holy City, Jerusalem, coming down out of heaven from God.* ¹¹*It shone with the glory of God, and its brilliance was like that of a very precious jewel, like a jasper, clear as crystal.* ¹²*It had a great, high wall with twelve gates, and with twelve angels at the gates. On the gates were written the names of the twelve tribes of Israel.* ¹³*There were three gates on the east, three on the north, three on the south and three on the west.* ¹⁴*The wall of the city had twelve foundations, and on them were the names of the twelve apostles of the Lamb.* ¹⁵*The angel who talked with me had a measuring rod of gold to measure the city, its gates and its walls.* ¹⁶*The city was laid out like a square, as long as it was wide. He measured the city with the rod and found it to be 12,000 stadia in length, and as wide and high as it is long.*

   ²²*I did not see a temple in the city, because the Lord God Almighty and the Lamb are its temple.* ²³*The city does not need the sun or the moon to shine on it, for the glory of God gives it light, and the Lamb is its lamp.* ²⁴*The nations will walk by its light, and the kings of the earth will bring their splendour into it.* ²⁵*On no day will its gates ever be shut, for there will*

*be no night there. ²⁶The glory and honour of the nations will be brought into it. ²⁷Nothing impure will ever enter it, nor will anyone who does what is shameful or deceitful, but only those whose names are written in the Lamb's book of life. ¹Then the angel showed me the river of the water of life, as clear as crystal, flowing from the throne of God and of the Lamb ²down the middle of the great street of the city. On each side of the river stood the tree of life, bearing twelve crops of fruit, yielding its fruit every month. And the leaves of the tree are for the healing of the nations. ³No longer will there be any curse. The throne of God and of the Lamb will be in the city, and his servants will serve him. ⁴They will see his face, and his name will be on their foreheads. ⁵There will be no more night. They will not need the light of a lamp or the light of the sun, for the Lord God will give them light. And they will reign for ever and ever.*

In December 1577 Francis Drake set off from Plymouth with orders from his queen, Elizabeth I. He was to sail to the Pacific Ocean, capture Spanish treasure from their treasure fleet and to claim any new territory in west of America for England. The mission was top secret; the orders would not have been written down for fear of provoking a war. It may have been he had a miniature painting of the queen in his ship. Certainly he would have had her command ringing in his ears. The voyage took almost three years. He lost four ships on the voyage, returning with only the flag ship, the Golden Hind. Yet the voyage was a brilliant success. Drake captured so much treasure that the Queen's share exceeded the government's income for a whole year. Drake claimed part of what is now the western U.S. for England (although the precise location was kept secret and is now lost). Nonetheless it was on this basis in the 17th Century that England could claim her Americas colony stretched from sea to sea. When Drake returned to Plymouth he was met by his Queen and knighted on the deck of his own ship. He also received a large share of the treasure, enough to keep him rich for life.

Imagine for a moment what it was like to be Drake in the middle of that voyage. There was desertion, loss of life, bad weather, no support. His world was his ship. It was a poor imitation of his homeland where the deck was a mockery of Plymouth's stable land. The food, instead of the rich crop of Devon's pastures was maggoty biscuit and salted meat. The company, instead of family and friends, was a motley crew. To sustain him there were his orders and his vision of the Queen, combined with the vision of the glory and riches he was bringing with him. When he returned to Plymouth he had no more need of the orders or painting of the Queen. The Queen was there in person. Here was glory in full regalia plus honour and wealth. He was reunited with family and friends and had his fill of all the good things of life.

Revelation 21:22 says this, "I did not see a temple in the city, because the Lord God Almighty and the Lamb are its temple". Throughout the scriptures the temple has been the place of God, the place where we can find him. Now we see there will be no temple in eternity. Why? The story of Sir Francis Drake is an imperfect human illustration of this. When the Queen is there he does not need her picture or to remember her orders. When he steps ashore he no longer needs the deck of his ship. The real thing is the whole point. Yet while he journeyed around the world, fulfilling his mission, these things were necessary reminders of the reality. So it is in the final chapters of the Bible. The Lord God himself and Jesus the Lamb are the temple. They are the real thing, not the world we see around us. That is only a poor imitation.

This is the dramatic change at the end of the scriptures. It has been mentioned many times already in this book because it changes how we look at the temple earlier in the scriptures. But does it not contradict everything else? There is an interesting comparison with Ezekiel's temple (Ezekiel 40-47) and the city in Revelation. Ezekiel's vision is also of the end-time, yet here there is a temple. What can we make of this contradiction? First of all, there are many similarities between John's vision of the city and Ezekiel's temple. In both there is an angel measuring with a rod (Revelation 21:15; Ezekiel 40:3-5); in both there are 12 gates at four points of the compass (Revelation 21:12-13; Ezekiel 48:31-34); both are "four-cornered" (Revelation 21:16; Ezekiel 45:1-5); both have living water flowing from them (Revelation 22:1-2; Ezekiel 47:1-9); both have trees with fruit and healing leaves on the river bank (Revelation 22:2; Ezekiel 47:12). We saw earlier that Ezekiel's temple was too large to be an ordinary structure; the city in Revelation is even larger, far too large to be an ordinary city. Its length (12,000 stadia, Revelation 21:16) is about 1,400 miles!

Nevertheless there are significant differences in Ezekiel's temple: there are still clean and unclean; the Gentiles are still separate; and most significantly there is still ongoing sacrifice. If Ezekiel's temple is indeed to do with the end times how does this fit in? Ezekiel's temple fits very well with the temple John saw in Revelation 11 where John himself is told to go and measure with a rod. This is the temple that exists in the heavenly realm now, after Christ's death and resurrection. It awaits the final judgement but it is in the midst of accepting the formerly unclean and the Gentiles (Acts 9 and 10). Revelation 21 and 22 are different. In these chapters we go beyond the end times that we are in now to the end itself, the final verdict and the restoration of Eden.

The overwhelming presence of God changes everything. Final change is what this last vision of the temple is all about. The temple is now God alone and he brings about whole scale change. He changes the physical world (a new heaven and a new earth, Revelation 21v.1). He changes us (nothing impure can enter the city, Revelation 21v.27). He changes the whole nature of life. The trees are the trees of life, their leaves are for healing and there will be no more curse (Revelation 22:2,3). This is reversal of the fall. The curse of humankind being ejected from Eden has become a new entry into Eden. The tree of life is there in its fullness and the healing leaves indicate that there will be no more death. "Now the dwelling (tabernacle) of God is with men, and he will live with them. They will be his people, and God himself will be with them and be their God." (Revelation 21:3)

So John is being given a vision of what that consummation will be like. It is one of the places in scripture where we begin to get a feel of the great hope we have before us. The illustration of Sir Francis Drake only goes so far. What can we get from this vision that is concrete about our future (whilst recognising that the vision itself cannot describe adequately the indescribable)?

First, central to everything, is the presence of God. This is above all. The vision expresses this by saying there is no temple; a central plank of the scriptures and of God's people through the ages is done away with. It is redundant because its purpose has ended. God is present in his fullness with his people. It is the failure of western secular society to downgrade the greatness of God. Christians from such societies easily fall prey to that cultural assumption. God is easily our friend but not so easily our King! At the centre of the city is the Lord and the Lamb. We see the astonishing nature of God: majestic yet a sacrificial servant, with the glory lying precisely in the sacrifice. This is our calling, to be like him.

Secondly one is struck by the sheer physicality of this new Jerusalem. It can be measured and has a size and shape. It has wonderful jewels adorning it. There is a new heaven and a new earth, with the new Jerusalem coming down out of heaven. Where is it coming to? In context it can only be coming to the earth. We are told it is coming like a bride, beautifully adorned, to her husband (Revelation 21:2). Once again if we take the context of the passage into account this can only mean those who inherit (Revelation 21:7), in other words the faithful followers of Christ. Although there is much symbolism in all this there is no need to doubt the real physical nature of God's recreation. It is reinforced by other scriptures, particularly the physical nature of Jesus' resurrection. The new Jerusalem is the new earth. It is God's way of remaking his world. There is a different image in Revelation 22:1-2, a vision of tree and a river which reminds us of the Garden of Eden.

Is the new creation urban or rural? It misses the point to be too specific. The use of both images is typical of a vision trying to describe the indescribable. The point of a city in the urban world (unlike today's western world) is that it was safe; it was the countryside that was dangerous. The wild beasts and the bandits existed in the countryside; the city had walls, authority and troops to keep them out. Yet in Revelation 21:25 we are told that the gates will never be shut because there is no night there. The glory of

God gives light and it would seem this glory and light prevents any danger or mishap from entering. Similarly the countryside is no longer a place of danger. There is no more death or sadness. The two images of perfect creation (the perfect city and the perfect garden) are simply images. No doubt both are true and both are untrue. The reality will be much more wonderful than we can imagine. Nonetheless what can be imagined is humankind, our own existence. It will be physical, a resurrection from the dead with resurrection bodies following the example of Jesus. His body was physical yet strikingly different (see the resurrection accounts in the gospels) and no doubt ours will be the same.

The fourth point about the new creation is the complete lack of suffering. There will be no more death or sadness. Whatever we have suffered in life will be removed. The effects of ageing or disease; the emotional pains of rejection or abuse; the congenital illnesses or self–inflicted harm; the suffering of poverty and starvation; the shattered hopes and destroyed dreams: not only will these be absent from the new Jerusalem, the past effects will be healed entirely. Revelation 21:4 and 22:1-3 leave no other interpretation. This is not only individual healing. It extends to whole nations. The western world may not underestimate the importance of the collective but God knows it exists and will heal there also. The effect of national peer pressure, when it is for ill, will be removed. There will in fact be one nation: the servants of the Lamb, who have their name on his forehead. For both nations and individuals the climax is this: death is removed. The curse of Eden is reversed and death is defeated forever.

There is one last point. Who exactly inherits all this? John tells us in different ways in these last two chapters. It is to those who are thirsty (Revelation 21:6) and those who overcome (Revelation 21:7). It is the nations and kings of the world (Revelation 21:24) thus including the Gentiles fully. It is the pure and those whose names are written in the Lamb's book of life (Revelation 21:27). It is those who serve him (Revelation 22:6). It is those who wash their robes (Revelation 22:14). This stream of descriptions in contrasted with two lists (Revelation 21:8 and Revelation 22:15) which describes those who behave against God's laws (murderers, the sexually immoral and liars) and who worship other gods (especially idols and the occult). Taken together this is a description of the true believer against the unbeliever.

The unbeliever is described in extreme language. Not all unbelievers are as bad as are painted in Revelation and nothing is said of those. How can we know who is saved? It is only through Christ, but his arm is long. Yet from this passage we can say that it is not everyone and many are not in the book of life. Instead they face the destruction of the lake of fire, the second death (Revelation 21:9)

However the description of the believer is typical of most Christians. The follower of Jesus is baptised ("washed"), pure (through Christ's sacrifice), thirsty for God, known by God (in his book of life) and ultimately overcomes sin, temptation and persecution (even if it is a gradual process). No Christian is perfect but all are forgiven. For those who feel unsure of their place in the book of life, the answer is simply to look again to the sacrifice of Lamb, who is at the centre of the new Jerusalem. The task for the Christian is simply to follow Jesus and await his return.

As we have seen earlier in Revelation, the good and just judgement of God will come from the temple, and then he will make all things new. There will be no temple because the Lord God and the Lamb will be fully present with his people and his creation. "Even so, come Lord Jesus".

### Questions to consider

Does the description of the believer sound like you?
Imagine what it will be like to be fully in the presence of God.

# Biblical Texts quoted at the head of each chapter

(with chapter number in brackets)

Genesis 2:8-12, 15-16; 3:24   (2)
Genesis 2:8-10   (15)
Genesis 14:18-20   (14)
Genesis 22: 2, 13-14   (17)
Genesis 28:10-19   (3 & 19)

Exodus 13:21-22   (16)
Exodus 24:1-12   (23)
Exodus 25:7, 18, 31   (2)
Exodus 26:30-27:1   (11)
Exodus 26:31-33   (18)
Exodus 27:20-21   (16)
Exodus 29:4-7   (7)
Exodus 29:11-14   (30)
Exodus 30:1-9   (5)
Exodus 30:11-16   (6)
Exodus 30:34-38   (5)
Exodus 30:17-21   (7)
Exodus 30:22-33   (8)
Exodus 31:1-11   (9)
Exodus 38:8   (7)
Exodus 40:34-35   (16)
Exodus 40:34-38   (27)

Leviticus 16:1-2, 11-34   (10)

Deuteronomy 16:2-7   (17)
Deuteronomy 24:1-4   (26)

2 Samuel 6:1-8   (8)

1 Kings 8 (extracts)   (4)

1 Chronicles 29:1-6   (25)

2 Chronicles 3:4-7   (9)
2 Chronicles 3 (extracts)   (11)
2 Chronicles 4:1   (11)
2 Chronicles 7:16   (9)
2 Chronicles 35:1-2   (17)

Ezra 3:1-3, 6   (25)

Psalm 51: 10-19   (30)
Psalm 110:1-4   (14)
Psalm 118:19-27   (21)
Psalm 137:1   (13)

Isaiah 6:1-10   (12)
Isaiah 42:6-7   (24)
Isaiah 53:7   (17)
Isaiah 61:1-3   (8)
Isaiah 66:1-2   (1)

Jeremiah 1:16   (5)
Jeremiah 7:3-15   (13)

Ezekiel 37:24-28   (20)
Ezekiel 40:1-5   (31)
Ezekiel 40:5-6, 17, 19   (32)
Ezekiel 43:4-5   (27)
Ezekiel 47:1-5   (31)
Ezekiel 47:1-12   (15)

Haggai 2:6-9   (29)

Matthew 2:11   (5)
Matthew 7:24   (25)
Matthew 16:16-18   (22)
Matthew 19:27-28   (23)

## The Temple